Trapped in a Diamond

SEVEN SIGNS THAT YOU ARE
LOSING YOURSELF IN A RELATIONSHIP

VITTORIA ADHAMI

Copyright © 2012 Vittoria Adhami

All rights reserved. Published in the United States of America. No part of this book may be reproduced or transmitted in any form or by any means, graphic, electronic, or mechanical, including photocopying, recording, taping or by any information storage or retrieval system, without the permission in writing from the publisher.

DreamSculpt Media Inc.
Sonoma, CA. USA

ISBN: Paperback edition: 978-1-937504-34-2
ePub edition: 978-1-937504-43-4
PDF edition: 978-1-937504-44-1

DSP 105

For more information, visit:
www.DreamSculpt.com
info@DreamSculpt.com

Book Design by Darlene Swanson
Cover Design by Howard Ronder

Produced and distributed for DreamSculpt Media, Inc. by BackOffice Publisher Services, Worthy Shorts, Inc.

To all the people who struggle to find the necessary strength to get out of an oppressive relationship, you have my admiration.

To my children whose courage facing adversities inspires me to be a better person and to my soul mate Giancarlo who daily nurtures my soul with his unconditional love.

Contents

Introduction ix

Part One

Chapter 1   Beaten But Not Defeated 3

Chapter 2   Opposites Unite. 23

Chapter 3   Stormy Weather. 39

Part Two   SEVEN SIGNS

Chapter 4   ONE: Your Needs And Wants Take Second Place 57

Chapter 5   TWO: Becoming Financially Dependent 65

Chapter 6   THREE: Living In Fear And Walking On Eggshells. . .73

Chapter 7   FOUR: Giving Up Your Personal Values 81

Chapter 8   FIVE: Afraid To Confront A Breach In Trust 89

Chapter 9   SIX: Too Apathetic To React To Your Losses. 97

Chapter 10   SEVEN: Your Personal Growth Is Ridiculed 101

Part Three

Chapter 11   Bicultural Marital Abyss. 107

Chapter 12   A New Life Chapter 119

Chapter 13   Loving Self, Loving Again. 123

Acknowledgments

My thanks also go to Jared Rosen my publisher who patiently put order in my thoughts and structure in my writing and to Judith Larson for a superb job editing.

Most of all I would like to thank the so many people I have met in my professional and personal life who showed me that giving up is never an option.

Introduction

I believe that all experiences in life are valuable. We can use the negative ones as lessons and the good ones as a reminder that we are on the right path.

This book is mostly for women who experience difficulties in their relationships due to differences in thoughts, values, culture or race. It is a book for women who, in order to feel loved and accepted, relinquish their freedom of thought and adopt their partner's thoughts and values. I am aware that men also can find themselves in the same situation, but it seems to happen more with women—that might have something to do with the conciliatory nature of women.

The loss of your sense of self can happen gradually without your awareness. The desire to be loved and accepted can blind you. It can be years, even decades, before you realize that your true self is lost or that you were never allowed to discover it. I intend this book to be an opportunity for readers who will identify with some or all of my experiences to find inspiration and encouragement to take their lives into their own hands. I will not give you instructions on how to act but rather make you aware of the signs that you are losing yourself in your relationship. I want you to find the courage to awaken your true self, which I assure you, will accompany you on your journey into the new life that YOU and only YOU will choose.

Throughout my life, I endured verbal, emotional, and physical abuse. I have been very fortunate to also experience real love and—most importantly—I have been able to forgive.

After the death of my husband, Cyrus, I discovered the secret life of my spouse, and at the same time, I realized that I had not only lost my husband, I had lost my past. The history I made with Cyrus had to be rewritten. His death was a tragic event, but the loss of my identity while I was married to him was even more tragic for me. I went through periods of hurt, doubt, discovery, forgiveness, resignation, and finally hope.

Throughout this time, I kept wearing a $40,000 diamond ring that my deceased husband had given me. I could not let go of it. But the mysterious loss of it one day was incredibly revealing to me. It made me realize that I had being looking at life as if from the distorted internal perspective of a many-faceted diamond. The loss of that ring changed my perspective on life, and I was inspired to write this, my first book: *Trapped In A Diamond*.

The only way you will surrender to someone else's will is if you are not sure of yourself and have no opportunity to discover your true self. Low self-esteem caused by events in your life may contribute to your inability to stand up for yourself. Many factors contribute to such inaction, but fear is the major contributor.

I will talk about experiences in my childhood, as I feel them to be the precursor of my action—or inaction—during the relationship with my husband. I invite you, the reader, to also revisit your own past and look for events that might have contributed to the fear you may have in your life. And I encourage you now to stand up for yourself.

Part One

Chapter 1

Beaten But Not Defeated

I was born in Italy in 1946, just after World War II. It was an exciting time in Italy. Free elections were held for the first time and democracy had triumphed. On June 2 of that year, the king was ousted, and Italy became a republic. I was born eight days later. I was born in a little town in the south of Italy close to a major city, Taranto. Our town had about 7,000 inhabitants including three to four prominent families, land-owners, and professional people. My uncle, the town doctor, and my grandfather, together with his brothers and a couple of other families, were the major land-owners. My grandmother's family was a prominent family of doctors and professionals. The rest of the people in town, with the exception of some artisans, were the workers of the land, the vineyards, and the olive groves.

My home town was located a few kilometers from the seaside town of Torre Colimena, where for a long time, we were the only family that enjoyed the free clams we dug on the beach. I fondly remember the days spent in the sun, wearing padded gloves, catching the sea urchins hiding between the rocks. We would eagerly go to our father for him to open them for us; we would then squeeze lemon juice on them and eat them, savoring the flavor of the sea.

After a month spent at the beach, my father liked to take trips and explore new locations north or south of Italy. I remember my mother holding the map, giving directions to my father, who often ignored her directions and got lost. I also remember sitting with my brother and sister in the back seat of the car and being annoyed by my brother, who wanted to sit by the window, but had to give it up because I suffered car sickness and had to be close to the window. He made me pay for it by pinching me and blaming me.

When I was born, my uncle, the mayor at the time, was convinced that my parents selected the name Vittoria for me because of the democratic victory in Italy in 1946. As a joke, he registered me as Vittoria Repubblica Italiana—literally, Vittoria Italian Republic. The reality was that my grandmother's name was Vittoria, and it was customary at the time to name children after their grandparents. Regardless, I was officially on the books as Vittoria Repubblica Italiana. It wasn't until I entered the educational system that the mistake was revealed, at which time my name was changed to Vittoria Anna Antonia Rosa, reflecting my grandmothers' names, step-grandmothers' name, and then some. I can see now that even from an early age, on some level, everybody had their own idea of who I was or should be.

My father and mother were educators. Both parents were democrats and very involved in politics. They taught during the day and devoted most of their free time to social activism. They lived a life of privilege and had the means to hire a housekeeper, a gardener, and a nanny to take on the mundane details of domestic life. In my parents' eyes, none of these activities were noble or the least bit pleasurable, so they delegated such tasks to others—including the care of their children. They spent very little time with us, except perhaps on holidays.

Until the age of seven, I enjoyed the privileged life and looked forward to the rare occasions when I would receive attention from my father. I was a pretty child and had been gifted with a good singing voice. From an early age, as young as three or four, I was often asked to sing in public and perform in the local plays at school. I remember playing the role of a lost orphan and memorizing quite few pages of script, unusual for a child of that age. It is ironic, now that I look back on it, that I played the role of an orphan. That was how I felt being with my parents. I loved those opportunities to make my father proud, singing at his club or on a stage, but they would soon come to an end.

Kidnapped

On my seventh birthday, while my father was making a speech at a political gathering, I was playing with some friends some fifty feet away. For some reason, we were unsupervised at the time. A man approached us and offered us bike rides. I took my turn with excitement, as would any seven-year-old child, innocent of the fact that his intention was to kidnap me. The man kept me for several hours; I wasn't located until the police and my uncle found me sleeping soundly on a bench in a bar where the man who abducted me had been drinking. I was later told that my abductor was a communist and committed the act to threaten my democratic father.

I remember the abduction with fondness. I wasn't a bit scared; I was excited to get a bike ride on a man's bike, sitting on the horizontal bar. It was night, and he took me a bit out of town. Maybe I should have been afraid, but I was having so much fun going fast on the bike, bouncing as the bike traveled over the uneven surface of the asphalt. He talked to me and asked me if I was having fun. I remember laughing aloud, as if

I were taking a ride in a carousel. This was such a contrast to what happened next.

Several hours later, (when I had been found by my uncle and the police) - I was returned home. After my uncle and the police left our house, my father started to beat me while asking me questions I could not answer and demanding information I could not give. He wanted to know if I had been touched in certain ways. When I answered no, or said something else he didn't want to hear, he continued to beat me. I was very confused, so I said no to everything and never disclosed that my abductor had touched my bum while lifting me from the bicycle bar to prevent me from falling. In my innocence, I knew that disclosure might have been interpreted differently, and I would have received more beatings from my father.

I was in shock. I had no idea what I had done wrong. I did, however, understand what I clearly saw in my father's eyes: his hatred for me. I knew then, beyond a shadow of a doubt, that I was no longer his little girl. My mother tried to stop him, but she was unsuccessful and maybe a bit afraid of him as well. She told me that when my father got really upset, he was not able to control his fury. Many times during my young life, I witnessed him being that way with my brother and I. At that time in Italy, it was not a crime to beat your children; it was the most common method of discipline.

I remember exchanging bedrooms with my brother. His room was next to my parents' bedroom. I was having nightmares every night. I remember that period of time and the nightmares very well. I would dream about being asleep in bed, when a gypsy would quietly come into the room, sit on my bed, and watch me for a while before covering my face, wrapping me inside my blanket, and taking me away. I would wake up screaming. Most times, my mother came into the room and sat on the bed, touching my arm to assure me that everything was okay and that it just was a dream. I must have awakened her with my screams, and she had run into the room. Or, maybe she stayed in my room for many nights, just making sure that I was all right. She knew the possible damage the kidnapping event could do to me, and she was sorry that she had not protected me before the event and after with my father.

After that first seemingly endless beating, nothing remained the same. I now lived in fear. I was terrified of my father. I felt unloved, ashamed, and damaged. At the time, I couldn't understand my feelings; I knew only that somehow I had disappointed my parents. My father stopped showing me off to his friends. There were no more trips to the cafe for ice cream. My voice, which had once rejoiced in song, was silenced.

I remember hearing my parents come home late at night, hoping they would stop by my room to tuck me in or kiss me goodnight. It never happened. Kisses were reserved for birthdays and for midnight on New Year's Eve. I have only one memory of falling asleep in my mother's arms, when I was five or six. It was a wintery night, and I felt her warmth on the front of my body as the fireplace warmed my back. I held this memory close to my heart, longing for another moment like that one, but it never came.

A few years after the kidnapping, we moved to the big city: Rome. My brother and I received beatings from my mother when she felt we weren't following her instructions properly. As I see it now, she must have been very frustrated. Inherently, she was a strong and independent woman, bound by marriage to my controlling father. She was a feminist living with a misogynist. Perhaps she, too, was living in fear.

My Parents

My parents loved each other very much. They were openly affectionate with one another, and we never heard them fight. But, they did not express their affection for us children. I remember feeling that something was not right. Why didn't they kiss us or hug us as they did with each other? Over the years, I have tried to make sense of my parents' behavior—not to justify it, but to attempt to understand it. It was the nineteen fifties, a period in society when beating children was more or less accepted though not to the extent they did. My parents were brought up in an age of fascism, so perhaps this helped to explain it as well.

My mother had experienced her own hardships. She lost her mother at the age of four and her father when she was seventeen. She attended boarding school from age seven to nineteen. The rest of her family lived in the US, too far away at that time to have any real connection. She, too, experienced very little warmth and affection in her childhood. When she met my father, he became the central figure in her life, and he demanded her full attention. He convinced her that he was her only priority and that her time was exclusively his. Perhaps this is the reason he insisted that others look after his children. We were very grateful to have a nanny whom we loved.

My mother's older brother was twenty-three years her senior; my mother was born when my grandmother was fifty-four years old. My mother refers to her birth as something her mother was ashamed of because it proved she had sex at her age, something of a taboo at that time. It was the early 1920s in a small town in Italy.

My mother had a privileged life until her father died. Then, she had to take care of herself, so after she finished her teaching certificate she went to work immediately teaching in a school and giving piano lessons.

She was a good pianist, and she believed that all women should be independent. It was during the time of fascism in Italy, and everyone was required to contribute to the state.

My parents married in 1942 in the middle of the war. Post-war, there were four political parties: Democratic, Communist, Fascist and Republican. They became Democrats. My mother became involved in the community in every way she could. She wanted to become a politician like my father, who converted to Democracy after the war. He could not lose the spotlight, so my mother took second place. She campaigned for my father and got the necessary votes for the Democratic party and for her husband.

My mother got involved in the Rights for Women's movement and became the president of The Center For Feminine Rights in the Puglia region, which is the equivalent of a province in Canada or a state in the U.S. It did not last long, because my father did not like the attention she was getting and asked her to leave the position. Ironically, I recall listening to her rehearse her speeches and hearing all the nice things she was saying along with her recommendations about women's roles in the family and with children, which were contrary to what she was doing at home. Even as a child, I noticed the contradictions.

By living a privileged life, traveling with her father every summer to various vacation places in Italy and residing in a good boarding school, my mother's aspirations were not matched by what life had reserved for her. She wanted to marry someone who lived in a big city, who was a professional, and who would allow her to thrive in modern and open environments like the ones she witnessed in her travels and learned about from her girlfriends at the boarding school. Instead, she married a very handsome man who brought her to a little town in the south of

Italy. He came from a good family, but life in a small Italian town in the 1940s was far from what she had imagined. In Italy, the south was very different from any other place in Italy, especially if you resided in a small town where everybody knows everybody. Every move you made or any dress you wore was news that would spread throughout the whole town within minutes.

I was seven or eight years old when my grandfather passed away. It was customary for close members of the family to wear black for a year. Men wore a black armband; women wore black from head to toe. My mother would not comply. The etiquette book said that one could wear grey, so for one year, she wore every shade of grey that existed, from almost white in the summer to almost charcoal in the winter. People in the town gossiped about this for many years, but she felt she had won a battle. She wanted to change all the old southern Italian customs, and she tried to change them one at the time. I am curious why my father allowed her to do this. He had lived outside the town to study, and maybe he was also tired of the old traditions. Nevertheless, this illustrates the rebellious actions of my mother. She could not win the war, but she was happy to win some battles.

My father was very much in love with my mother and knew that her life with him fell short of her expectations. He worked very hard to get out of the little town and move to the big city of Rome. My mother knew that if she did not obey my father and satisfy his need to be the priority in her life, she would not be treated well. He had made it clear, in that small community, that even though she worked and earned the same amount of money he did, he was the head of the family. It was very important for him to have his wife always next to him and always available, with no interferences. And we, their children, were interferences.

Paolina's Departure

Our beloved live-in nanny, Paolina, also joined us in Rome. I always considered her to be my real mother. She was the protector, the caring human being we so desperately needed in our lives. Paolina was always there for us, trying in vain to stop the beatings and consoling us afterward. At age forty-two, Paolina fell in love and left us to marry a wonderful man in northern Italy. We were devastated, but at the same time, we were delighted for her.

Her departure changed my life dramatically. I was sixteen and my older sister was nineteen. The newest additions to our family were a five-year-old and a two-year old. With five children, a career, and no knowledge of cooking and cleaning whatsoever, my mother's efforts to run the household on her own were disastrous. A housekeeper was hired to work every day for five hours to contend with household chores, and I became the care giver of my younger siblings.

My mother knew nothing about mothering and had no desire to learn. My older sister somehow escaped her responsibility toward the little ones, so it was up to me to be their mother, their friend, and their playmate. I enjoyed it, possibly because it was the first time and only time I felt loved. My parents took full advantage of this, and as they gave me more responsibility for the children, they took away more of my freedom. To say my needs were secondary is an understatement. I simply wasn't allowed to have any.

My father and mother entered parenthood believing their children should be coerced, manipulated, and forced into the mold of who they wanted them to be. As a result, our ideas were ignored, invalidated, or ridiculed. "You still have milk behind your ears," they often told us. "You don't know anything about anything." Those words pretty much extinguished any freedom of expression or trust in our own inherent wisdom. Our biggest conflicts were about political and religious issues, and about personal freedom to express ourselves. We were forbidden from making any negative comments about anyone who was a Democrat or questioning our religious beliefs.

Between my care-giving role and their strict rules governing my social life, I felt like a prisoner. As for our limited outside activities, we weren't allowed to go out with boys, and in my case, not even with girls. I was the babysitter. I could socialize with my girlfriends only on the rare occasions when my parents stayed home and only in a very limited way. The rules we lived by were so strict, I broke them every chance I got. My spirit had not been completely extinguished, and I had a rebellious streak.

I got into conflicts with my parents, most of which culminated with a slap or two from my mother or a full beating from my father. The most violent beating I ever received was the time my father saw me in a car with my boyfriend. I had long hair at the time, which he pulled as hard as he could as he beat me. He kicked me until my internal and external injuries were impossible to ignore. As the abuse continued, I was reminded of my first childhood beating and the confusion I experienced that terrible day. *The punishments didn't fit the crimes.* Grasping for answers, I often wondered if I might be adopted. Who was I really? It was the only way I could justify such violence.

Regaining My Power

Following that last beating from my father, I summoned all the courage I could muster and threatened to go to the media and the police with my story. Surely, my broken body held all the necessary evidence. After that day, my father never touched me again. My mother continued to beat me, however, whenever she was frustrated or not getting a desired response—until the day she beat me with a stick. I pushed her away and she fell on the bed. It was the first time any of us had reacted this way. I managed to escape to my sister's home and stayed there a couple of days, afraid of my mother's reaction. I had never put my hands on my parents. It just was not something a child could do to a parent. I had always taken their beatings with a straight face, never ducking the punches, always looking them straight in their eyes while they were slapping my face. It must have bothered them that I would not submit to them. Maybe that was the reason they would beat me more. They could not break my rebellious spirit. When I returned home from my sister's house, neither parent asked me where I had been nor was I never beaten again. I was nineteen years old.

Though the physical abuse had ended, the emotional abuse continued. Their private discussions were easily overheard, and I was well aware that they had no confidence in my intellectual abilities. "Vittoria is not that intelligent, and we need to think about how we can get her a job," they would say with resignation. But I had a teaching certificate and held tenaciously onto my own inherent wisdom that I *was* intelligent. By this time, I had lost all respect for them, both as parents and even as knowledgeable people with good judgment.

Fortunately, I was blessed with friends—wonderful, intelligent, educated, and caring women friends my mother's age—who believed in me. They were always there to encourage me and to remind me that I was a beautiful person inside and out. I shared with them all the ideas that my parents had ridiculed. Thanks to them, I was able to establish a certain level of self-esteem. One of these women lived in the same building I did, and my parents never realized the extent of the influence she had on my life. I can say with certainty that I owe my life to these women.

As a young woman, I wanted to change the world. I didn't believe in the existing political and religious institutions. I believed strongly in the equality of men and women and abhorred favoritism toward men. It was a strongly patriarchal society, and having two brothers, I directly experienced how differently the genders were treated. Even at the dinner table, the bigger prime cuts of meat would be dished out to my father and my brothers first. They were strong men and need more energy. My brother was also given much more freedom. Just one year my senior, he was allowed to go out with whomever he wanted and to return late at night. I, on the other hand, was not allowed to attend parties until I was eighteen. But again, I was rebellious and was able to escape from time to time.

When I was sixteen, I managed to go with my sister and cousin to an adult party. There, I met the first man who would turn my head. I received what, at the time, I interpreted as pure love from this man who was almost double my age. He made me feel wanted, loved, and cherished. And he wanted to take me away from it all. Seeing me in his car prompted that last and most violent beating from my father. Unfortunately, the relationship was not destined to be. My parents strongly disapproved, as he was of the Christian Orthodox faith. We were able to keep our relationship secret for a couple of years, but eventually he had to return to his homeland of Greece.

I had many conflicts with my parents over our different ideas about religions and social classes. At one time, they hired a girl my age as live-in help, and I was greatly saddened by the way they treated her. She couldn't eat with the rest of the family or go to a movie with me. She wasn't even allowed to talk to me much or to be seen with me in the street. My parents were still playing the part of the prosperous and elite family from the south of Italy. They remained untouched by the social revolution that had swept the country and much of the rest of the world. Given my restrictive upbringing and my parents' prejudices, it's a miracle that I managed to develop my own very open and progressive views and values.

Singing My Song

Through it all, my passion for singing never abated. A songbird in a cage is still a songbird, and I longed to sing. Instead of being encouraged, however, my love for singing was almost destroyed. I had a good soprano voice, and the women who were my guardian angels encouraged me to pursue a singing career. I begged my father for voice training until he finally agreed, and I had an audition with a very famous teacher. At the end of the audition, my father asked the teacher what he thought about my possibilities of a career as a singer. He asked, "Can she be a Callas?" Of course, the only honest reply the teacher could give was, "But there is only one Callas." As we left the studio, my father turned to me and said, "If you can't be a Callas, you can forget about singing." My heart sank, and I felt something die in me.

Fortunately, I got another chance at singing when I earned my teaching certificate and decided to get a diploma as a choir instructor. This gave me an opportunity to sing as a soprano in the school choir. The choir toured several theaters in Rome and the surrounding cities, and I enjoyed it very much. Sadly, my family never came to any of the performances.

Like many teenagers, I was curious about everything. I had an insatiable need to discover and learn. Religion was something I struggled with, and I couldn't accept the Catholic Church's answer to all my questions, which was to "have faith." Every time I needed a difficult question answered or a situation explained the answer was always the same: "Just have faith." I came across some information about the occult, and because the Church forbade the practice of it, I pursued it all the more enthusiastically. I went through my stage of spiritualism, séances, and hocus-pocus of all kinds, but even with these explorations into the unearthly realms, my mind, body, and soul still felt imprisoned. Countless restrictions and constant criticisms weighed heavily on me. It was as if I was bound in chains. I felt an undeniable need to escape. Somehow I knew that if I didn't, Vittoria would die.

Mercifully, a door opened. My parents wanted me to find a job, and they agreed that learning English, along with my Italian and French, would be helpful. I did my research and found a place in London that was supervised by nuns, the only place away from home that my parents would have let me go. The only aspect I didn't like was the 9:00 p.m. curfew, but freedom from my current situation was well worth the sacrifice. Because the nuns would have control over me, my parents agreed to the idea. But ultimately, destiny had other plans.

A relative from Canada, who was my age, visited us in Rome while on her honeymoon. When I told her of my plans with the nuns in London, she proposed an alternative: *"Come to Canada and live with me while going to school!"* I was overjoyed at the prospect and thought my parents would embrace it as well. Of course, they had countless reservations, particularly regarding the distance from home. I pleaded with them, threatening that I would run away and shame them. I don't remember what else I said, but I finally succeeded. I soared away on October 31, 1966, with no idea of where I was going or what I was getting into. I did know, however, that it was my flight to freedom—a little scary, but oh so exhilarating. I had heard that life in North America was very different.

There were no strictly defined social classes, everyone had equal opportunities for jobs, and everyone was entitled to be treated with respect. I was going to a young country—merely one hundred years old—which stood for the values I held so dear. Everything there would be brand new. *Anything and everything* was possible.

Cyrus

I arrived in Toronto and was soon enrolled in the International Institute for English. Little did I know I would learn so much more and embark on a path I never could have predicted with a man I was apparently destined to meet. It wasn't long after my arrival in Canada that I met Cyrus. We had a brief and silent exchange in front of a vending machine—a glance and a smile. Cyrus arrived in Toronto a couple of weeks after me. He came from Germany after escaping from Iran where he worked for the security of the Shah making sure that the equipment was in order. As such, he was not allowed in the 60s to leave Iran without special permission, but he managed to do it without being caught.

Since birth, his life had been a continuous battle to survive and to acquire self-esteem. Cyrus and his family felt they had lost self-respect when his father's gambling habit cost them all their money. All his life, Cyrus worked very hard to accumulate wealth. He thought money would give back self-respect and dignity to the whole family. He spent all his life believing and proving to himself and everyone else that hard work makes everything possible. His life was incredible, full of adventures and ups and downs.

Cyrus was born in Kerman, a city in the south of Iran with a population of 100,000 in the 50s and over 500,000 today. He was born into a very wealthy family. He enjoyed telling with pride the story about his father's car having #1 as a license number and the police having #2. It was the same with their telephone numbers. His luxurious life lasted until he was seven years old, when his mother died of cancer. When I asked him about his memories of his mother, he told me that at her deathbed, she asked to see her son for the last time. As he entered the bedroom, his mother asked him to give her a kiss. She touched his forehead and told his sister to take his temperature, as she taught he had fever. He was moved that her last words were of her concern for the well-being of her son. He became very emotional describing the event; it was the last memory, or maybe the only memory, he had of his mother. It had taken a few years to gain his trust before he shared this memory with me.

Cyrus's sister, nine years his senior, substituted his mother in taking control of the household while his father continued to gamble. A couple of people, faithful to the family, continued to help with the housework. Cyrus's older brother, who had married while their father was still wealthy, never helped, even when times were very difficult for Cyrus and his sisters. After his mother died, his father became depressed. He continued his travels to control his properties, but he got more deeply involved in his gambling habit. He lost all his properties and most of their precious possessions. His father was also a very kind man; Cyrus fondly remembered him returning home on cold nights without his coat, because he had given it to some beggar in the street.

Due to his father's bad habits, Cyrus had to witness the richness of his relatives while daily confronting his poverty. Most of his father's poker partners were relatives, so the wealth changed hands but stayed in the family. Cyrus was determined to dedicate his life to getting out of his precarious financial situation and overcoming the sense of insecurity his childhood experiences had given him. His most desired goal, besides achieving financial security, was to gain the trust and respect of every individual he would meet. And for that, he would do anything as long as it was legal.

At fourteen years of age, he was entrusted by his cousin to lead a full caravan of camels, jeeps, and thirty men to transport opium through deserts and mountains. At that time, the production and sale of opium for medicinal purposes was allowed. As a fifteen or sixteen year old young man, Cyrus took his father to Tehran, trying to find a cure for some mysterious disease I have never been able to learn the truth about—some kind of insanity caused by sunstroke, they say. Cyrus remained in Tehran and brought his sister to live with him as well. She was several years older than he, but in need of a place to stay. She was a single, beautiful woman who, in a country like Iran, needed to be protected and watched, as she apparently was a bit of a rebel.

Cyrus's father died when Cyrus was seventeen, making him an orphan taking care of himself and being in charge of an older sister. After a few years of working various jobs to survive, he finally contacted a cousin who was a general in Shah Phalevi's army. Learning about what had happened to Cyrus, his cousin was happy to help him find a job. He started as a mechanic, and in Cyrus's style with his complete dedication to any task that was presented to him, he became the person in charge of the vehicles in the escort of the Shah. It was a very good position, but it did not pay enough money.

He decided to open a taxi business: he bought a car and hired a driver. When Cyrus was working at his day job, the driver would drive the taxi, and Cyrus would drive it at night. The business became relatively lucrative. His ambition was to get rich and get an education. He knew that only by leaving Iran could he succeed at both. After the second marriage of his sister, when his responsibilities in Iran were considerably reduced, Cyrus fulfilled his dream of leaving Iran for Germany where his friends were waiting for him. They had gone to Germany before and were encouraging him to do the same.

Europe in the 60s was an exciting land of opportunities, and with the help of his friend, a colonel in the army who had a German wife, Cyrus embarked on one of his great adventures full of expectations and dreams. He traveled with the colonel's wife and two young children, one less than two years old and very fond of Cyrus. When they went through customs, by accident or destiny, the little girl was sleeping in Cyrus's arms. The officer mistakenly believed Cyrus was the little girl's father and stamped the passport with a special permission, which allowed him to stay and work in Germany. Opportunities, freedom, and challenges were there for him. All that he wanted was there for him to take, and he did.

He went to school and worked. He learned German and enrolled in a technical school to become an aluminum specialist. He worked in an aluminum foundry and was promoted to a management position within a few months. He loved his position, but not his job. It was very hard, working ten hours a day in a very hot environment. He earned good money, but it was not what he wanted to do. An accident in the foundry killed a friend, and that made him think that he should get out of that dangerous job. A friend from Iran, Eric, had been with him in Germany for a while but had decided to go to Canada where it was easy to emigrate. Unknown to Cyrus, Eric applied for his friend to go to Canada also; he even signed the application forms, and in no time Cyrus found himself accepted as an immigrant to Canada. It was November 1966.

Our children listened to his stories, fascinated by his experiences in a faraway land, captured by the intrigue. Every Sunday, our family sat at the table from 11:00 a.m. until 2:00 p.m. for brunch. We would discuss issues and tell our children stories of my childhood in Italy, of Cyrus's life in Persia, and of the Persian Empire, Darius the Great, the war with Alexander the Great, and Persepolis. These were names of people and places I heard about as a child, and I was fascinated by the history and the mysteries.

Cyrus would talk about the flat peaches and the exotic fields of pistachios and saffron. We were all transported with our imaginations into the fields of poppies from which the opium was extracted just before dawn. When Cyrus described the early morning harvest of the opium, we were all there with him. He was a good storyteller!

Chapter 2

Opposites Unite

Sometimes, I had doubts about the validity of Cyrus's stories. No one person could have had all the experiences he had in his short life. But his family confirmed most of his stories. Hearing about opium and caravans was new and fascinating for me. It was a world I had only known through history books or magazines. I had in front of me a portion of history, a first-hand account of costumes and experiences in faraway lands, and I loved it. He spoke about a life of danger, intrigue, and adventure. I couldn't help feeling distant from it, but at the same time so captivated by the stories of his life.

It was the opposite of what I had experienced in my life. I had lived a much protected life, and drugs were only mentioned in very low voices by adults. They did not want to expose us to such a vulgar or corrupt world. Even though there must have been illicit drugs used in Europe, I did not hear about it. Only street people used drugs. My first exposure of Italians using drugs was in the early 60s watching Federico Fellini's film, *La Dolce Vita*.

I was twenty years old when I arrived in Canada. I had never made my own decisions or handled money. I was not given the opportunity to choose my own education. My parents decided that I had to become a teacher, just like them, and that was it. I wanted to frequent the International Institute of Languages to learn new languages, maybe work at the United Nations, be a translator some place, or work for an airline. But that was not acceptable to them. Women should teach so they could have a family and be at home with the children when schools were closed, and that was that. I also wanted to be a singer, and that was not accepted either. I had no choice, so I became a teacher.

I also could not buy my own books. Every year before the school year started, all my friends would get money from their families and they would go together to buy their books for the school year. It was an exciting time for them. But I was not given such a pleasure, as my father was in charge of that. My parents did not trust our judgment, and they definitely did not trust us with money. Then, all of a sudden I was alone in Canada, forced to take care of myself and to make decisions for the first time in my life. I had never before had the opportunity to learn, to make mistakes, or to have someone to guide me. Of course, I made many mistakes when I was left on my own. Being unsure of what to do, I was always asking myself what my parents would do in the situation I was in. Even away from them, my low self-esteem did not allow me to use my inherent wisdom. Fear of failure controlled my decision-making.

Trust: His Blueprint and Mine

Cyrus and I were two wounded souls in search of an escape, in search of a dream that would make everything all right. We were both looking for unconditional love, respect, and success. Our reasons for our quests might have been different, but our goals were the same. We confronted our life challenges from different perspectives.

We all have our own blueprint for the word *trust*. My life experience should have made me more distrustful of people. I could not even trust my own parents! I chose, though, to trust everybody, as I could not make sense of being betrayed by my own parents. Logically, I thought my parents' behavior was rare, maybe even unique. Maybe my experiences with them put me on a search to validate my idea that almost all people are better than my parents, and I needed some confirmation that was true. I trusted all my relationships until proven otherwise. I gave people all the benefit of the doubt that I could. I believed that there must be a better world out there waiting for me and that I could trust everybody to help me fulfill my dreams. I believed that people were inherently good, and that if you approached them with a pure heart, they will respond with goodness and love.

I trusted Cyrus implicitly and ignored all the signs that I should have seen. His blueprint of protection included control. I should have listened to the hints he was giving me that I was not enough for him, that he needed more. He had never been in a serious loving relationship with a Persian girl before marrying me, and he felt there was something missing, but he was not sure what. Maybe he was looking for what he had been exposed to in his culture, to legally have multiple women.

Cyrus's life experiences taught him to trust no one. Maybe he was older and, as they say, "a pessimist is an optimist with experience." Well, that was what he chose to be. He was never completely exposed, he always wore a shield, he approached everybody with a fair amount of mistrust, and he put everybody to a test. I suppose he did that with me as well. He trusted me, maybe more than anybody else. I believe now that I must have been the only person in his life he truly trusted. Ironically, it was his illness that caused him to open up with me fully. He told me that he knew from the moment he chose me that he had made the right choice, that I was perfect for him, and that he felt unconditionally loved by me: Too late for me.

I showed him throughout our life together that no matter what, I was there for him. When he had to confront death, I was with him twenty-four hours a day, going through despair, hope, and surrender. But it had not been this way before. To the contrary, he had often made me feel I was not good enough for him: I was too short, too mouthy, too western, too fat . . . but, "I love you anyway," he would say. Those were not very encouraging comments for my self-esteem.

His appreciation of my constant presence during his final journey and my full dedication to him made him finally feel secure enough to expose his insecurities to me. He reported all the injustices he had received and described how he overcame the numerous challenges presented to him as a child and throughout his life. He apologized continuously for the pain he might have given me in my life, and he gave me hints about the pain I would have after his death.

Intuitively, I realized that I would find out about things that would pain me, and I told him that whatever they were, he did not need to ask for forgiveness—he could be sure that I had forgiven him because I loved him. It felt so good to forgive, and I am glad I told him how I felt. And, at that time, I meant it. I did not yet know what I had to forgive; it all came to the surface after he died. After his death, I felt lost, alone, fragile, and scared. Who would I trust now? Would I trust again?

Middle-Eastern Love Song

Christmas preparations at school had just begun, and I volunteered to sing the Bach/Gounod "Ave Maria." Just a few weeks after our encounter by the vending machine, Cyrus sat in a nearby classroom and heard me practicing. Unlike my father, he was immediately impressed with my voice. In fact, he fell in love with it. Gathering his books and leaving the classroom, he followed the sound of what he would come to call the "angel voice." When he opened the door and saw me singing, he knew—then and there—I would be his wife. We hadn't exchanged a word, but his mind was made up. I was his woman.

He pursued me with a couple of invitations for trips outside of Toronto. I'd lived a very sheltered life up to this point and rightly felt I should proceed with caution. I didn't want to leave the city with a man I barely knew. After politely refusing the second time and preparing to explain I'd prefer to meet him at a café in Toronto, he hung up abruptly before I had the opportunity to explain myself. As I heard the "click," I had the odd and heavy sensation I had lost something very precious.

After Christmas break, I changed schools and continued with my English classes. Months later, as I entered the cafeteria one day, I heard a familiar male voice. Just across the room, I saw him. Cyrus! As he began running toward me, a force heretofore unknown to me propelled me toward him. As we met in the middle of the room, we embraced and kissed, as would two lovers meeting after a long separation. The entire room erupted into applause and cheers, like a scene in a movie.

"Where were you? How have you been? How are you? Why didn't you call?" Words, English words, spilling from our mouths like notes of a brand new song sung for the very first time. We talked nonstop, showing off our newly acquired language skills, eager to communicate for the first time, to give love its expression. Classes were about to start, but we were oblivious of everything but each other. Nothing else was important. We left the school grounds and walked the streets of Toronto, holding hands and gazing into each other's eyes, savoring the sweet miracle of our serendipitous reunion. Thus, our relationship began. Every day we met at school and our ritual continued.

Two weeks later, Cyrus invited me to meet his friend in Scarborough. Two bus trips and one subway ride later, Cyrus introduced me to his friend as his wife-to-be. "We plan to marry in June," he said, in a matter-of-fact tone. I was stunned and unable to hide it. Our relationship had started just two weeks prior, and the topic of marriage had never arisen. I became increasingly confused and angry, but remained a courteous guest and kept my cool. By the time we left Cyrus's friend's house, my cool and courteous demeanor had reached an end. I could contain myself no longer. "How could you do that?" I asked. "Why didn't you discuss it with me first? What is this, a Persian custom? You choose the girl you like and you take her if she wants it or not?" He apologized, but explained that he was sure about his feelings and figured I was as well. I repressed feelings of anger and betrayal. We kissed and immediately made up. When passions are at play, reason is gone with the wind.

Another two weeks passed, and we had been together for nearly a month. It was time to introduce me to another friend, a German fellow who taught English at the school where we first met. We were to attend a party where we would meet many people. While climbing the narrow staircase to his friend's house, Cyrus whispered excitedly in my ear, "We will tell everybody we got married a month ago!" Before I had the chance to respond, the door opened, and we were surrounded by a crowd of people.

They all seemed happy to see Cyrus, but their smiles faded instantly when he introduced me as his wife. I was in shock and accepted a glass of wine. Soon, I was pulled into a room where several women asked me questions about when I had met Cyrus, how long we had been together, and when we got married. They seemed to be struggling with the timeline. I appreciated their interest, but it all seemed so strange, almost surreal. I didn't want to disappoint Cyrus, so I answered their questions the best I could. At the same time, I was struggling to repress my anger toward him. There he was, laughing and drinking away with his male friends, leaving me to fend for myself during this inquisition with a story he had fabricated.

Their initial demeanor when I was introduced as his wife and their reactions that followed made me uncomfortable and confused. It became evident that they were trying very hard to hold back tears. They were not tears of joy. A couple of them left the house, and I was finally able to approach Cyrus and challenge him about the ridiculous charade. I was clearly upset and felt terribly manipulated.

It was quite late, and I wanted only to go home. I expressed my thanks to our host, but offered no further goodbyes as I left. Realizing my state of mind, Cyrus followed close behind, telling me I should be happy and grateful to him. He had arranged the evening especially for me. All the women at the party had been his girlfriends with whom he had intimate relationships during the time we were apart. This staged arrangement was his way of letting go of his bachelorhood and committing himself to me for the rest of his life.

The proper response for me would have been to run away as fast as I could, but love is blind. All I could see was an ardent twenty-nine-year-old man promising to love me for the rest of his life. I immediately melted into someone or something that was unrecognizable to me. I called it love. We made love that night for the first time, and it was beautiful. Throughout, he declared his love, whispering in my ear, "I want you to be the mother of my children." I think I touched heaven for the first time in my life. It seemed so real, so pure, and so clear. I was loved. He had been right all along. I was going to marry this man.

Breaking The News

I waited until my twenty-first birthday to tell my parents of our marriage plans. I was deathly afraid they would come to Canada and take me back to Italy. I was terrified I would lose my love—my ticket to heaven—forever. I wrote them a letter, explaining I had met a wonderful man. He was not Italian, nor was he Christian; he was Muslim from Persia. He did not yet have a job but was studying English with me. We would be getting married in September. I phrased the letter not to request permission but to ask for their blessing, which I would have appreciated but didn't need. I ended my letter with, "Of course, I would love for you to be here for the wedding."

I can only imagine the shock this letter caused my parents. Cyrus was without a job . . . and a Muslim? I lied and exaggerated about his education, telling them he would become an engineer in Canada, assuring them all would be well. The truth was that the Canadian government was paying us each thirty-five dollars a week to study English and this money was only available for a limited time. Surprisingly, they sent me a letter immediately, congratulating me on finding this wonderful man. Along with their well wishes came a suggestion that we enter into marriage slowly and take our time. Maybe we should go to Italy to live first and then get married. They not so subtly added that my former boyfriend, Milziade, was back in town and asking about me. I suppose at this point a Greek Orthodox looked much more promising than a Muslim.

It must have been very hard for them to accept my decision without having been informed or consulted first. In the Italian tradition of the time, the man would go to the woman's father to ask for her hand in matrimony, similar to North America. Not only did Cyrus not do this, but they were not able to find information about him and his family, as was also customary in Italy. Cyrus was from another country so far away and so different, it was not possible to investigate.

On the other hand, there was also a problem for Cyrus. In his culture, the parents usually choose a wife for their son. Sisters are also influential in the choices their brothers make; many times, wives are chosen by the circle of friends and relatives. Sisters try to find a woman who can be compatible with their brother and also with them, because in the Middle East or Muslim society, the wife is always seen as an outsider and therefore must have the qualities to fit in and not cause problems in the family's unity and harmony. Sisters also look for a woman whom they can control in some way. The bride knows that her position is secondary to her husband's mother and sisters because they are related by blood.

Cyrus did not follow the traditional customs; he made his own choice. When confronted in the future with his family's attempts to assert their traditional roles, he made it very clear to them that his wife came first, and I was very grateful as it avoided unnecessary conflicts.

Cyrus, too, sent his family a letter informing them of his decision to marry and introducing me to his family by including photographs. I conveyed my greetings to his family through his brother-in-law, who was an English teacher. I can only imagine their comments! Not only was I not Persian, but they did not choose me, and I was Christian to boot. I was an emancipated and unorthodox person, even according to my own western culture.

His family was overtly accepting of the situation, though some relatives did everything possible to sway him to the Persian way, putting him in an awkward situation. He defended my behavior and explained my western positions. The older, conservative members of his family must have found it difficult, while his younger relatives were more modern in their views.

Marriage Western Style

To my surprise, my parents agreed to come to Toronto and participate in our marriage ceremony. When they arrived at the airport, my gallant fiancé greeted my mother with a beautiful bouquet of flowers and a kiss on the hand. He won them over instantly with his gentlemanly ways. My mother was somewhat taken aback by the darkness of his skin, which hurt me, because of her concern over race and color, and also because Cyrus's beautiful skin tone was one of the many things I'd fallen in love with. In my parents' defense, their prejudice was founded on their lifetime lack of any contact with people of another race. In Italy, everybody was white except people from other countries who worked in the embassies. Ignorance was the cause of my parents' prejudicial reactions.

We were married in a civil ceremony by a Scottish clerk. It was difficult for any of us to understand much of what was said, but we were there to be married, so we said yes to everything. Afterward, we went to a restaurant for a late lunch. At the end of the meal, my father asked, "What time do we have to be at the church?" It was a very awkward moment. They had not asked, and I had not informed them that we were not going to marry in the church. Although we were both spiritual, and we had been raised Muslim and Christian, Cyrus and I were not followers of any particular religion.

When I replied to my father that there would be no church wedding, he was stunned. As he was about to express his disappointment, my mother intervened with a look—the same look she had used when my brother and I behaved badly in public. Words were never spoken on the subject, but my parents gave me a gift-wrapped box, which contained my framed communion certificate and a telegram from the pope along with his picture and signature. If you had connections in Italy, you could obtain these things, and my father had connections. They intended that the telegram would be read and the other items displayed at the church ceremony. You can imagine their disappointment. But that was that.

We started our married life with hope, love, and commitment. We had only a weekend for our honeymoon. My parents were going to Paris before returning to Rome, and their return flight departed from Montreal. We decided to take them to Montreal and to visit Expo '67. We visited the Persian Pavilion; Cyrus was so proud to display the richness of his country to me and my parents. I got very sick with tonsillitis, but I did not want to spoil the moment and said nothing about my sore throat and fever.

In the middle of the night, I started talking Italian. Cyrus was unable to contain my tossing and turning and my loud Italian voice. I was delirious from the high fever. He timidly knocked at the door of my parents' room and tried to say that I needed help. They initially thought that there had been some kind of trouble between us as a couple, but when they entered our room, they soon realized what was happening. The hotel called a doctor who immediately administered antibiotics.

My parents left for Paris, and we started our trip back to Toronto. Ordinarily, the trip would have taken six hours. Unfortunately, it took much longer. The doctor in Montreal recommended that I drink plenty of liquids. On the way to Toronto, we stopped at a gas station. Due to Cyrus's and the vendor's limited English (in Quebec they speak French), he returned to the car with apple cider vinegar instead of apple juice. I was sleepy and in so much pain that I attributed the sour taste to my sick taste buds and I drank the fluid. After drinking a cup or so, I could not drink anymore, and my stomach started to feel upset. The vinegar may have been good for disinfecting my tonsils, but it was not good for my stomach. It was raining profusely, and it took three times longer than usual to finally arrive in Toronto just in time for Cyrus to leave me at home and go to school to take an exam.

The Honeymoon Wanes

Cultural differences between us soon became evident. Our discussions evolved into disagreements with raised voices, which evolved into arguments with us swearing in our respective native languages. As soon as we were frustrated about something, our command of English decreased, so we reverted to the languages that were easiest for us to express. For our English-speaking neighbors, still my friends after forty-five years, our discourse seemed peculiar and funny. When we were very angry, we would make up swear words, translating literally the idiom *drop dead* as "fall down dead" or *go to hell* as "I hope you go to the inferno."

Cyrus soon learned some swear words in Italian from an Italian school friend, and he used them without knowing the level of vulgarity he was speaking. His friend purposely taught Cyrus certain words to have fun with him, not knowing that he was using them with me. When I told him the real meanings, he stopped using that language immediately and reverted back to his native tongue. After arguing about everything in our first year of marriage, he said, "I know that sometimes you might disagree with me, but I do not want to know your disagreement when we are talking. Please say yes and agree with me at the moment. You can tell me the truth about your thoughts at another time. You do this, and I promise you everything will change." And so I did. I could not stand the fighting anymore; I tried his suggestion and it worked. He thanked me for following his instructions, and we had fewer discussions and fights for a while. It was his first attempt to control me.

My mother had given me the same suggestion the night of my wedding. She wanted to talk then about sex, which to me it was unnecessary and unwelcomed from her, but she did suggest that I respect my husband. For her, respect meant not confronting your partner in a conversation, rather to agree with him even if you really don't, and to reason with him at a different time. I suppose in some ways it had worked for her. For me, following this advice meant silencing my thoughts and ideas.

This was the first thing I gave in to Cyrus. Fear was my reason. Every time someone raised their voice, I was sent back to my childhood memory of my father and that terrible beating when I was seven. Cyrus did not know about that part of my history: I tried to show him that I was cool, sure of myself, able to look after myself, and didn't need anything from anybody. Had I been more secure and mature, I would have been able to deal with the situation in a better way. I would have been able to tell him about my fears, and I am sure he would have been more sensitive. Instead, I would either surrender or counterattack, which escalated the conflict.

I have recently become a teacher of Powerful Non-Defensive Communication (PNDC). I teach people skills to improve their communication in conflict or when one is put in a defensive mode. I regret that during that time in my life, I was unaware of different ways of communication. As Sharon Allison, author of *Taking the War Out of Our Words*, would say, I was using the "War Model" of communication. When in conflict or when put in a defensive situation, we counterattack, surrender, or withdraw. Just like in war. But, I was very young, a person in development who needed to work on myself and to have someone who could understand me and help me un-tangle the convoluted web that had grown around my young life.

The Woman Behind The Successful Man

Cyrus finished his English classes and earned the equivalent of a high school diploma, and he was very happy. He thought that with some education all doors would open, but he was wrong. He had to find a job, and the economy wasn't great at the time. After trying and failing many times, I tried to convince him to become an insurance agent like I was at that time. He strongly rejected the idea, but finally he gave it a try. The company would pay him a basic salary while he was training, and then he could earn commissions. The manager decided that I would be his trainer. Every night, he accompanied me while I met my potential clients. This proved awkward, because he did not speak Italian and my clients knew very little English.

Cyrus was very intelligent, and by observing me he learned much of the Italian terminology for selling the product. Some of the clients spoke English well enough to converse in both languages. After about two months, sitting in the car in a client's driveway, I informed him that he would speak with the client and I would observe. I had been telling him for a while that he had to start, but he would always say, "Next time." I knew he was ready.

We stayed in our car for more than fifteen minutes with him refusing to go solo. Out of frustration, he punched the windshield, which completely cracked. He refused to go in. We returned home with the broken windshield, risking an accident. We did not talk to each other for a couple of days. I knew he was a very proud man, and having to depend on his wife for financial support, or any other kind of support, was unacceptable. But, I knew I had to push him to act.

He was a very smart and resilient man, and after few days he proudly came home one evening having sold his first life insurance policy. He presented it to me and proudly said, "I don't need you anymore." He thought I would be upset, but I was happy—that was my objective in the first place. All of a sudden, he had found his calling. The Italian people accepted him with open arms, trusting him more than they would an Italian man. With the little English they knew and the little Italian he knew, they were able to do business together. He became the most successful agent in the company, maintaining that status for the twenty-five years he worked in the industry and qualifying every year for the Million Dollar Round Table, the highest award in the industry.

His clients loved him, and he did his job brilliantly. While he was building up his business, I became pregnant with our first child. During the pregnancy, I worked for the Berlitz School doing English-to-Italian translations for products' labels. My son was born, and Cyrus was successful in his new profession. I continued to translate until my son was fifteen months old; I then went to work for the federal government, first as a clerk and subsequently as a fraud investigator officer with the proper training and badges.

I felt great. But my heart broke every time I had to wake my son up at 6:30 a.m. to get him ready for nursery school. I needed to work to save money toward buying a house. I worked until the eight month of my pregnancy with my second child. Cyrus really wanted a second child. I wanted a child myself as well, but I knew that I could be away from work for only six months. After that, I could not go back to my previous position. I had to want another baby very much to leave such a great job, and I did.

Cyrus had made many business connections, and he began to sell insurance policies to Iranian professionals. His success allowed us to have another child and me to be a stay-at-home mom for a while. We agreed that I would stay home and take care of the children for the first five years of my second child's life. After that, I could go back to work.

During my married life, I had many years of pure joy seeing my two children grow into beautiful human beings. I also felt their love for me, and that was enough for me as a mother. When put in a position where I had to choose between my children or myself, without a moment of hesitation I chose my children, even though I was aware that it meant I might be silenced forever. I never regretted the choice. I thought at the time that I had no other choice. It was a conscious choice. But there were limits. I could not accept infidelity.

Years passed quickly, and we were celebrating our twenty-fifth wedding anniversary. I considered myself lucky. I thought I had it all. Certainly, there had been some bumps in the road. I had forgiven many things, I thought the worst was over, and I believed we were going to live the rest of our lives happily together. Cyrus planned to retire in a couple of years. We intended to travel the world together while waiting for our children to marry and to give us grandchildren and everything else that would come with it.

Chapter 3
Stormy Weather

It was the summer of 1992, and we were going to have a summer of special celebrations: our twenty-fifth anniversary, my brother's twenty-fifth anniversary, my parent's fiftieth anniversary, and my niece's wedding. The children and I went to Italy about a month before Cyrus. We all went there to celebrate, but the celebration turned to tragedy.

When Cyrus arrived at the airport, I noticed his skin was darker, but I thought he had taken some sun. His legs were swollen, but we attributed that to the flight: he had swollen legs a few times during the previous nine months, but the doctor said that his checkup results were good and he should eat less salt. He was tired, and we attributed his fatigue to the flight. Then, he became feverish, and we thought he caught a cold or something. It wasn't long before hepatitis B was detected in his blood.

Cyrus was diagnosed in Italy with severe cirrhosis of the liver caused by hepatitis B, which he contracted long before but had gone undetected, even during his annual checkup in May just a few months before. We learned later that the doctor had failed to notice the elevated enzyme numbers on the liver test. If the doctor had not overlooked those results, Cyrus may not have had the symptoms he had in July. We will never know! He was one of the unlucky ones among those with hepatitis B:

only one per cent of people who contract the virus fail to form antibodies. A liver transplant can be their salvation. But, we later learned that even with a transplant, in Cyrus's case the survival time was limited.

How could this happen to him, to us, to our children? We were in Italy to celebrate; it was supposed to be a joyous time. Always careful about his health, Cyrus exercised every day, ate well, didn't smoke, and didn't drink except wine occasionally. How did he get hepatitis B? Why didn't his doctor see signs of it in the blood test during his annual physical? We had the best help and medical expertise in Italy. They concluded that Cyrus's liver was so cirrhotic, only a transplant would help. He was too weak to travel. We waited a couple of weeks, and then we returned to Toronto.

When we arrived in Toronto, we soon saw Cyrus's doctor, who was surprised at the situation. We were very angry with him for overlooking the lab results, but we needed to act soon. All the tests Cyrus took in Italy were requested again, and the results compared to the ones taken in Italy. It was confirmed—only a transplant would help. We approached the medical authorities responsible for transplants, eager to learn the date of the operation so that the problem could be solved.

To our dismay, they sat us down and told us that even though Cyrus needed a transplant, there weren't enough livers in Canada for all who needed them, and they could not spare available livers for people who have hepatitis B. If Cyrus had been an alcoholic, it would have been okay. After a transplant, an alcoholic stops drinking; everything could be all right. But with hepatitis B, the virus was in the blood; therefore, the chance that the virus would return and destroy the liver was very high. We left the meeting with an imminent death sentence: Cyrus could survive two or three months, maybe six.

Our lives changed in an instant. No more hope. Until then, we felt despair with the news of his illness, but we had hope that something could be done. Now there was only despair. "Canada does not have enough livers to spare" continued to play over and over in my mind, like the screeching noise of a malfunctioning merry-go-round. Canada did not have a liver for my love, the father of my children.

What about the rest of the world? What about the U.S.? It is a big country, and everything is possible in America. We called the Mayo Clinic, New York, Boston—all the best places that performed liver transplants. The Deaconess Medical Center in Boston was the first to reply. "Yes, we have received your request. Come to Boston and we will take the necessary tests to analyze the situation." They were the sweetest words we had heard in a long time. In a matter of a few hours, we collected all the medical documentation from Italy and Canada, and we went to Boston. Cyrus was happy. He regained some hope. I was reminded of his life motto: "Everything is possible in life if you want it and work hard for it." Cyrus died October 11, 1993.

Transformation

From the moment his disease was diagnosed, I entered an intense and overwhelming period in my life. I was not prepared. I think no one can be truly prepared. I was with Cyrus twenty-four hours a day, sharing every emotion with him. I became something of a nurse, giving him daily injections of interferon. Every injection gave him severe flu-like symptoms that would last for hours. It was very painful for me to be the one to give him pain, but the hope that it would help gave me the courage to do it.

The moment he was diagnosed and understood the severity of the disease, he surrendered to me. All of a sudden, I was elected to be in control of everything—the family, the finances, and his life. I was overwhelmed. I left to Cyrus all the medical treatment choices, even though he always tried to get me to decide. I was trying to give him some control over the event that swept our lives. We would discuss the issues as they presented themselves, but the final decisions about following a certain path, taking medications, or having an operation were all up to him. I was there to support him in whatever choices he made.

He chose always to try everything recommended by his doctors, no matter the pain and discomfort. Near the end of his life, when the doctors said that there wasn't much that could be done, he answered. "If you say that there is not much that can be done, there must be something possible even if the chance of improvement is minimal." His doctors proposed the terrible injections of interferon, something he dreaded, but they told him there was a five per cent chance it would work. He said, "Five per cent is better than zero." Cyrus never lost hope and he fought to the end. His motto was, "Everything is possible in life if you want it and work hard for it."

It must have hurt him a lot to finally realize that wanting something and working hard for it doesn't necessarily assure that you obtain it. There are so many other factors that play into the equation of life. I believe that if you want something in life, if you work very hard for it, you increase the chances of getting what you want, but it does not guarantee that you get it. That Cyrus had overcome so many terrible things in his life made him believe that he could control all the elements in his life. It was the force that allowed him to overcome tragedies and injustices, and he really believed he was invincible. How hard it must have been for him to be defeated.

I distinctly remember the moment I was transformed from an insecure and fearful person into a confident person. We were at the Boston airport on our way back to Toronto to settle our affairs so that we could return to Boston for the liver transplant. The flight was delayed three hours. Cyrus started to act crazy; he was speaking Farsi, but in a way I could not understand. He was irritated, trying to push me and not wanting to sit in the wheelchair, which was necessary because he was not able to keep his balance. I learned later that it is typical for patients with liver decease to have these episodes when the bile is invading their organs and brain. I was alone, pushing the wheelchair while he was trying to carry on his lap a briefcase containing all his medical documents.

I realized the severity of the situation, and I did not know what to do. Cyrus had made most of the decisions in our life, and he was definitely not in any state to decide now. I literally and clearly heard a voice in my head. It was like my brain split in two: the old Vittoria and the new Vittoria. On one side was the old Vittoria who retreated when someone raised their voice and quickly complied with the aggressor for the sake of peace and fearful of consequences. On the other side was a Vittoria that literally started to hear a new, loud, firm, strong voice in her brain saying, "It is up to you. Do what you want. Don't listen to him. Do what you think is right."

Cyrus wanted to continue on to Toronto. I decided to go to a hotel, ignoring his requests to turn the wheelchair around and board the plane. We went to the hotel, deposited the suitcases, and I called for an ambulance. I was unaware that in Boston at that time, if the patient didn't agree, the paramedics could not transport the patient to a hospital. It was after 1:00 a.m. and I was desperate. I called the transplant surgeon, but to no avail. And then, fortunately, I remembered that a doctor who extracted fluid from Cyrus's belly the day before had given me a phone number with instructions to call him at any time if there were complications. I asked him to talk to the paramedics and explain that he was on the waiting list for a transplant. They accepted him into the ambulance and he did not show any resistance.

The doctors at the hospital told me that if I had not taken Cyrus to the emergency department, he would have died within a few hours. Needless to say, saving his life felt great but I also felt a sense of empowerment. I felt capable to make decisions—important decisions—on my own, firmly and resolutely. I knew I had turned a page; a new Vittoria was born. I knew I was strong, I knew I was capable, and I knew I did not need anybody to approve my decisions. From that time on, there was nothing that could stop me; I was in control of my life. My strength came from finally making a conscious decision to take control of my mind and my life.

Greatest Journey

My greatest journey had just begun. I was accompanying Cyrus to his death. The highs and lows began to manifest. It was a seesaw of hope and despair. Cyrus had so much hope and trust in the transplant operation. Throughout his illness he showed incredible dignity. He worried about the nurses who would see him suffer and might be disappointed with his progress. He would ask me to comb his hair, shave him, and help him into his elegant housecoat because he wanted to take a walk twice a day down the hall to the nurses' station. He would smile and say hello, and then go back to his room and collapse on the bed, exhausted. The nurses admired and appreciated that very much, and they gave him compliments about his attire. He always greeted the doctors and the nurses who came into his room with a big smile, even when the news was not good or he was in pain.

Every afternoon, Cyrus waited for his doctors' 3:00 p.m. visit when they talked about his condition after reading the daily blood tests. When the news was not good, he consoled the doctors, whom he loved because he felt they cared. He would touch his doctor's arm and say, "It is not your fault. You will see; tomorrow you will bring better news." He was able to establish a very special relationship with everyone involved in his care. For months after his death, I received notes from his care givers about how touched they had been by us as a couple and by his behavior as a patient and as a man, and that knowing him had made them better care providers.

To the end, Cyrus showed his appreciation for work well done. He admired people that worked very hard, regardless of the job they did. Sometimes, I noticed that he would purposely do something the hard way, as it would give him more satisfaction. He knew no shortcuts. He felt more rewarded if the job he did required harder involvement. His illness humbled him, and he was grateful that he was finally free to be vulnerable. He felt safe enough with me to tell me the secrets of his life as a child, his thoughts, his fears, and his hopes - which had been crushed many times.

He realized that he had finally found the unconditional love he so desperately searched for. He recognized it in my love, and in his typical proud way, he would say, "I knew I made the right choice the moment I heard you singing and decided you would be my wife. I am so sorry things have been difficult for you, and I am afraid they will be more difficult in the future. You don't deserve that." He might have referred to things I would find out after his death, things he was not proud of and would hurt me.

Cyrus was a teacher in my life. As a husband, he made mistakes and he hurt me. As a man, he has been an inspiration. From him I learned determination, work ethics, perseverance, to follow the light at end of the tunnel, to aim high and never give up, to accept defeat and to rise up again, to believe in myself, and to hope. He showed strength and fortitude of character to the end.

The day before he died, something happened that helped me to forgive him after I discovered the truth about his double life. When the doctor told me that there was no hope and that Cyrus could die in a few days, I chartered a jet to bring Cyrus to Toronto where all his Persian family members were waiting. Cyrus had been in coma for a couple of days, and the nurses had just prepared him for the flight. My children were also in the room. Cyrus took all the strength he could muster, sat up in the bed, opened his eyes, and said, "I love my wife, I love my children." Then, he went back into his coma and never spoke again. The nurses were shocked; we all hugged and cried.

How important it must have been for him to say those words to me and to his children—so important that he came out of a coma to do it. Only Cyrus could beat the odds to be able to come out of a coma to say what was on his mind. It was a declaration of love and redemption, and a statement about the essence of his soul, who he really was, who he had become, and what he had realized was important in his life. I tried to remember his words every time I felt despair about his betrayals, and I wanted so desperately to forgive him. It took a long time, but I finally did. I chose to remember him as he had become at the end of his life instead of making his memory out of a small portion of his being.

Redemption

I tried all my life to find a reason to love my parents. I was raised as a Catholic, therefore "honor your father and mother" was a very important commandment, and I believed that in order to honor them I must love them. Why did I not feel that love? Was I a sinner? As a child or teenager, I had never heard of parents abusing their children. Nowadays, this kind of news is common. I suppose at that time it existed, but we would not hear about it in the media or from people we frequented. I tried to hide the abuse, not because I thought I caused it, but because I felt ashamed that I had such terrible parents.

There have always been conflicts between parents and children. My parents' generation was taught to parent like their parents, but in my generation, there was a revolution of thought. Freud and Jung were very popular, but Dr. Benjamin Spock's child-rearing ideology was the bible. Maybe it was the first time in history that the children expected something very different from their parents. While social revolution was happening, with the advent of new media and new philosophies, our parents were stuck on the old definition of parenthood while the new generation had expectations that were not embraced by the majority of their parents. The consequences were evident in the strong generational conflicts of the 60s. It was very difficult for parents, but some adapted and succeeded to have a balanced relationship with their children. Others, like my parents, failed.

It was also a cultural matter. We noticed that the south of Italy strongly resisted the changes, while the middle and the north tried harder to change and succeeded. In addition, it was a matter of character, of putting children as a priority, and that was never the case in my family. I made up my mind that to free myself, I had to forgive my parents no matter what. What made it easier with my father was his recognition that he had made mistakes.

I never heard my mother say she was sorry or recognize that she had some responsibility for what happened in my life. She was the enabler of my father's abuse. Even though she was also intimidated by his behavior, as children we wanted her to defend us, or at least be the person we could go to for consoling after the beatings. We always saw her as an accomplice to his acts. She adopted the same method of discipline my father used, beating my brother severely until age eleven when he finally became much bigger than she. My beatings consisted of a slap or two to my face when I said or did something she disapproved of. She preferred to slap me with the back of her hand; she would say that would be more painful for me so I would learn the lesson better. Many times, she forgot to take her rings off and the slaps resulted in cuts to my mouth or face.

Many years later, when I was a mother of two children, my parents came from Italy to visit. I needed to confront my father about the way he had behaved toward me during my childhood and teen years. I reminded him of the episodes in my childhood and the beating he gave me when I was eighteen and he caught me entering my Greek boyfriend's car. He could not remember the kidnapping, but he remembered the other times he beat me. My mother did remember the kidnapping and agreed with me that my father had been too violent.

At that time, I accepted that he did not remember, but now I think that he must have felt so ashamed of his actions that he could not admit to me openly his past cruelty for fear of altering the harmonious relationship we had been able to establish between us in my adult life. My father had become a much calmer and warmer man, and before allowing him to be close to my children, I was able to observe his transformation and be sure of its sincerity.

Even though my father did not remember everything, he did apologize, which was healing for me. But, what made me forgive my father and free myself of the resentments I had about the pain he caused me was something that happened during my parents' visit. Cyrus was on the floor playing "horsey" with our children. Down on his hands and knees, Cyrus was carrying them on his back, letting them fall off from time to time, bursting with laughter. We were all laughing, except my father, who was crying. We asked what was wrong and he said, "Please forgive me. I did not know how beautiful it could have been for you and for me if I had played with you when you were a child." I didn't know what to do. My father had never played with me. His own mother died when he was four; probably no one had played with him.

I embraced my father, kissed him, and told him that it was all right and that he was forgiven. I felt so relieved. A big weight had been lifted off my shoulders. He had finally said what I wanted to hear for so many years: "I am sorry." Seeing a man in his sixties become aware of his mistakes, knowing that he can never get back the time he lost, and being vulnerable enough to expose his weakness and ask for forgiveness was enough for me to turn that page in my life. We were two adults sharing the pain of our life together, and this was the first time I had ever kissed and hugged my father with deeply felt love and forgiveness. From that day forward, I witnessed my father's transformation into a wonderful grandfather for my children, whom he loved dearly.

I have learned to never dwell on the memories of the past or let them seep into my present relationship with my mother. I learned that forgiveness is a liberator of the spirit. My parents developed great, loving relationships with my children, who still today have great affection for them. I am very appreciative of this and very happy that my parents had the opportunity to create wonderful memories for my boys. They took them all over Italy, and they had the opportunity to learn about each other. The best of my parents is in my children's memories. For this, I will be forever grateful to them.

After my father's death, my mother has become the sweetest old woman ever. She has transformed herself into a docile, enthusiastic, active person. She plays the piano every day, entertaining the seniors in the retirement home where she lives. She organizes groups for outings and participates in the university studies about old age and the brain. She confessed to me that at ninety-one years of age, this is the happiest she has ever been. I suppose this is the first time since her youth that she has been able to be herself again and to be in control of her life.

With Cyrus, redemption came simultaneously with his illness. He needed someone to lean on, and after long reflection about his life, he had finally realized that I had always loved him unconditionally, and that he could finally, for the first time in his life, trust someone totally. And he did. I was his rock, and I promised myself to be there for him, strong until the end. He profusely praised me for my past and present actions and for who I was as a woman, a mother, and a wife. I thought that hearing the words I wanted to hear all my life would make me feel good and fulfilled, but everything was so bittersweet. It was enough to forgive him, but so sad because I knew that he was dying soon and there would not be enough time to rebuild our relationship and enjoy the transformation.

Freedom

The morning classes were going to start momentarily. I was approaching the classroom when... oh, my God! I forgot my diamond ring in the bathroom. I knew it... I knew it! When I took the ring off and put it on the counter to wash my hands, I knew something wrong would happen. I had never taken my ring off since 1982 when Cyrus gave it to me on our fifteenth anniversary. Okay, there was time to get to the class and come back to the washroom. I will find it there for sure. Oh, my God, it's worth $40,000 and I have never been without it. I put it on my finger every morning and took it off at night. I never took the stupid ring off even to wash the dishes. It was a cardinal rule: do not take the ring off your finger in a public washroom. Why did I take it off?

I felt surprised I had taken it off, but I also felt like it was an action I did not participate in consciously. It was as if a force outside myself directed me. I don't know how to explain it. I was talking to myself while I was taking my ring off: "What are you doing? You never take it off—especially in a public washroom!" But I took the ring off nevertheless, promising myself not to forget it after drying my hands. I started talking to myself again: "I never took my ring off at a public bathroom! What came over me? Okay, okay . . . I am at Harvard Law School taking a mediation course with judges and lawyers from all over the world . . . Come on Vittoria, someone found it and gave it to the lost-and-found. Take a deep breath; use all the techniques you know. Come on, you are a life coach and a hypnotist. What do you say to your clients when they panic? Yes, take a deep breath . . . another . . . inhale . . . 1-2-3-4 . . . exhale . . . 1-2-3-4. What if a student took it? Yes, there are some students here in the summer, and I remember seeing a cleaning lady around. They might be desperate and not give it back."

I opened the washroom door and didn't see the ring where I thought I left it. I looked on the floor. I put my hand in the waste paper basket. I looked again . . . up . . . down . . . nothing. I ran out of the washroom to the information desk. The course organizer who was in charge of the whole group was there. I approached the desk, my head exploding. I was short of breath as I told her what happened and I asked her if she would please tell all the instructors to ask the students if they had found a ring. She assured me she would do that. I turned my head and saw the door to the communications room open. Someone was there, amid the wires and cameras, and I told him what happened. He suggested I go to the lost-and-found and gave me directions; it was about two hundred yards from our building. I prepared myself to go down two flights of stairs; I had no time for the elevator. My leg muscles didn't help me much. I was in shock.

"Okay, Vittoria . . . it is just a ring. You are not going to have a heart attack over a ring. No, no is not just a ring! It has so many meanings for me beside the value. Wow, $40,000 gone down the drain. *Mamma mia*! I can't even think that it has been stolen. It will show up, for sure. Take it easy . . . breathe in . . . 1-2-3-4 . . . . and out . . . . 1-2-3-4." I arrived at the counter of the lost-and-found room and told my story. They advised me to wait until tomorrow when all the maintenance people would have reported to the office. "Okay. Of course, the cleaning people . . . maybe someone cleaning the bathroom . . . yes, I remember some cleaning people near the bathroom . . . or maybe not. I don't know any more, I can't think straight."

I decided to go to class. Erica, our instructor, was letting the class do introspective exercises and meditation. "Yes this is what I need . . . not really! I don't know what I need! Why did I take it off? Why? I don't know." Then something happened. I started thinking about Cyrus, the ring, Boston, and everything strangely started to make sense. Why—really—was I in Boston?

Why Am I in Boston, Really?

Tony, my collaborative-lawyer friend, had encouraged me to become an associate of her practice. She told me about the mediation course at Harvard, and together we joined the large group of mostly judges and lawyers attending the summer session. For the prior fourteen years, I had wanted to return to Boston, as I had unfinished business to take care of. I knew I needed closure after the death of my husband. I thought going back to Boston where he spent the last eight months of his life may be the right thing to do and that was the right time to do it. I had the support of my dear friend, Tony.

I planned to go to the Deaconess hospital, visit the room where Cyrus stayed for so many months, and meet with his doctors and nurses. I was discussing this with Tony the night before the disappearance of the ring. Boston represented for me a place of sorrow, anxiety, desperation, and pain. It was also a place where I felt I had finally become aware of my strengths and I where, for the first time beside the time I nursed my children, I felt needed, essential, and wanted. What a paradox. I was there to save my husband but he with his situation was rescuing me. I don't know if I threw the ring with the paper into the paper basket, if someone actually took it, or if by mysterious intervention, Cyrus took it away from me to allow me to examine the meaning that ring had in my life and why I was so attached to it. It really did not matter; I was forced to review my life, my relationship with Cyrus, my personal values, and to discover who I really was.

I am writing this book because I don't want anybody who might identify with my story to make the choices I made in the past. My fragile soul, hurt by my childhood experiences, had clouded my decision making, and I found myself following a path designed for me by others. I want you to take control of your life and to turn up the volume of that inner voice that is continually trying to tell you to speak out, to be strong, to have a voice, and that you count and are precious just because you are you. It is a matter of increasing the volume and shutting off the other voices that say otherwise. Don't look for unconditional love outside yourself; give it to yourself first, and then you can spread love around you. I realized that MY head is on MY shoulders, and therefore it belongs only to ME. A simple deduction, and yet it took me so long to realize it. It had always been there, and I could have used it any way I wanted at any time, and yet . . .

In Part Two, I want to share with you the memories I have of times and events during my marriage that I now see as signs that I was losing myself and becoming someone else's idea of a woman. If you let someone else dictate what you think or do—for whatever reasons, justified or not—you risk losing yourself. I have identified seven signs that I was denying my right to be myself. Some are subtle, others may be evident to an observer but not to the principal actor.

Part Two – Seven Signs

Chapter 4

One: Your Needs and Wants Take Second Place

A few months after we began our marriage, I was hired to work for a bank. Unfortunately just few days before I started work, I fell and broke my wrist. We didn't have government insurance yet, and we had no money to pay the hospital expenses. The doctor who treated me was very sensitive. He put the cast on me, and I paid fifty dollars for the use of the hospital facilities. To save me money, he suggested I go to his office in six weeks to have the cast removed, and I agreed to that. But, he did not have the proper instruments in his office. He decided to make the cast extend from my hand to just below my elbow. He proceeded to cut it diagonally with an electric cutter, and then he secured it by wrapping tape around it. He thought that would suffice.

Because I was working as a bank teller and had to count money all day, my wrist wasn't healing and needed adjustment from time to time. The doctor repeatedly removed the tape, readjusted the cast, and wrapped it again with adhesive tape. After three months, he told me that if I kept using my hand, I would have permanent damage. I went home crying, and I was very worried about our future. I earned fifty-five dollars a week; Cyrus earned thirty-five. It was just enough to pay our expenses. If I stopped working, we would have been in serious financial trouble. Or so I thought.

When I told Cyrus what the doctor said, he replied not to worry, he had some money put aside, and I could stop working until my wrist healed. He was so proud to be able to say this, but I had a complete opposite reaction which I did not verbalize. How dare he let me work in pain with a broken wrist, worried that I could lose the use of my hand? What heart does the man that I love have? I could not stop thinking, "Why?" He is generous, loving, and caring. What would make him behave in such a way? Why would he not tell me we had some money? I started thinking of reasons to justify his behavior. Very odd, but I did. Perhaps, I thought, it was too early in our relationship for him to trust me.

During my married life, when I wanted to buy furniture or paintings, I was never allowed to. If I wanted to purchase an expensive item, I had to ask Cyrus's permission. It was out of the question for me to see a beautiful painting and just purchase it. He did not appreciate the value of it. One time, I wanted to buy a painting I really liked that cost $850. It was a beautiful semi-abstract painting of a woman's body. Cyrus liked the painting, but he said the painter was not famous and it was too expensive.

A couple of months later, he came home with a small silk Persian carpet, which he hung on the living wall. When I returned home, he asked me to close my eyes because he had a surprise for me. He took me to the living room and showed me the surprise. I was so hurt. I felt I should not disappoint him and graciously thanked him. Then I went to my room and cried. I realize now that it was his way to manipulate me to accept his will. He knew the value of a carpet; he spent $3,000 on it. But $850 for the painting was a waste. I could not assert myself, I was afraid of his disapproval and disappointment.

When we would travel to Italy in the 80s, I'd see beautiful jewels in the store windows and give many hints about what I liked and what would be nice to get me as a birthday or anniversary present. I never got those jewels. Cyrus would get me more expensive gold and jewels from Iran. He thought that all his Persian friends would know how much he loved me by how much he spent for the gold he bought me. No one knew how much the Italian jewels cost.

He did the same thing with the car. He came home with a Ford Mustang, and presented it to me as a gift. I had no say about which car I would have liked to drive. He did all the research and decided that it was a good car and that I would like it. Here we go again! It was exactly what my parents did with me when I was a teenager. They bought my cloths, my books, and choose my courses. I had to be thankful and not complain, because if I did I was an ungrateful person. And so I felt with Cyrus. I didn't say anything, I did not think I had the right to complain or say what I wanted. I felt I should be grateful that, as he said, my friends would give an eye for what I was getting from him. I went from the frying pan into the fire.

While I was in the hospital delivering my child, Cyrus's cousin, his cousin's wife, and their six-year-old child came unannounced from Iran to visit us. My husband welcomed them with open arms and gave them the use of our bedroom. When I came home from the hospital, I had to sleep in my son's room with the new baby. I have traveled around the world, and I think the Iranian's hospitality is the best, though at times excessive. In their culture, guests come first, even before the comfort of a man's wife.

This was too much for me. My husband left me with a new baby, my older son, and the six-year-old child of his cousin. I had to deal with my sons, one just born, and babysit for another child who could not speak English, while they all went to New York and Montreal. I did not like that, but his guests were more important than anything or anybody.

This behavior was unheard of in the western world. I attributed his behavior to cultural differences, but it was also his need to show off that he had money, he could do whatever he wanted, and that he could leave everything and take his rich relatives on a trip to New York and Montreal to buy fur coats. I was very upset—I had expected his participation in the care of the new child. I should have had more help upon my return from the hospital, not more responsibilities with a child I could not communicate with.

I did not voice my discontent about the situation at the time, because I knew he felt guilty. He was caught between doing what was right for his wife and satisfying the expectations of his countryman. He chose the latter. His cultural ties were very strong, and he must have thought that he could make it up to me in some other way. When they returned, they thanked me for taking care of their child, and I was given a mink stole as a gift. My husband thought that made it all right. Later, I tried to discuss the situation with Cyrus, but I did not finish my first sentence before he raised his voice, saying that I could not understand because I was not Persian.

I thought that if he married me that meant he trusted me. I interpreted the episode about my wrist and the secret about the savings as lack of trust, and I believed it was my fault for not showing him he could trust me. I thought the onus was on me to demonstrate to him that I was trustworthy. I was reacting to the lack of trust my parents showed me.

They always interrogated us children, and even though we spoke the truth, they would tell us that we were lying. We were told to go to our rooms and come back with the truth. When we came back with the same story two or three times, they would finally accept it. Sometimes, to end the charade I would say something I thought they would like to hear just to stop the process. This, of course, made me believe that they were not interested about the truth but only about their truth.

I made excuses for Cyrus's behavior, trying to defend him. There was no reason for not trusting me. But, was trust the reason he would not share financial information with me or was there some cultural factors influencing his behavior? In his culture, financial matters were, and still are, never discussed with women. Women did not go to the market to buy food, the men did. Men controlled the money and women received an allowance to buy something for themselves. Cyrus was doing just that. Keeping a secret about his savings was normal for him.

I came from a different experience. In my family, expenses were decided together by my father and my mother. The only arguments about money I ever heard was when my father wanted to buy a new car every two years and my mother would not agree to it. My father won this argument most times. We knew that financial matters were always discussed and they were coming to an agreement. I was with a man who behaved as if his way was the only way. I felt insecure about financial matters; I had lived alone for only one year while he had been in charge of himself for fifteen years. I allowed him to be in control, but I thought he would consult me more. He didn't. I did not want to rock the boat. If I made suggestions or requests, he would not consider them or he would criticize them. I backed away and let him do what I thought he knew best.

There was another cultural factor which I observe happening in many cultures. In Iran, men bought expensive jewels for their women to show how successful they were. The bigger the diamond, the richer they were and the more important they felt. In many cultures, women are seen as showpieces. In the Iranian Muslim culture, money also has an unusual function: it permits men to have four legal wives and infinite concubines or temporary wives. More money equals more women—legally.

Some cultural differences can be about things other than money. In some cultures, women are considered equal partners while in other cultures, they are not: they are possessions. Women, wanting to be welcomed and included, may not want to upset their spouse's family and their traditions. A woman might put her wants and needs secondary just to get along, to be accepted, and to be loved. She might refrain from questioning certain beliefs, as merely questioning them might cause conflict or put in question acceptance by her in-laws. A question or critique of a particular traditional way can cause suspicion regarding her commitment to the relationship. Not being knowledgeable of the culture, she may be very cautious not to disturb it while also having a kind of reverence for it. In our case, for a wife who came from a modern European society and a husband who came from a more traditional, sometimes a bit tribal, background like Iran, the differences were distinct.

I understand now that in Cyrus's case, his lack of trust in me was in part the result of past experiences he had with other women who took advantage of him. The last serious relationship he had before me was with a German woman he took to Iran to introduce to his family as his future wife. She was a journalist who wanted to write an article on Iran, and she took advantage of his generosity. While all his family members were showering her with gifts of jewels and Persian carpets, she was writing about her adventure in Iran to her German boyfriend, informing him that she still loved him and that Cyrus was "just a thing." Cyrus found the letter, packed all the gifts she had received, took her to the airport, and sent her back to Germany. This was his experience with western women. He could not trust them, as they had betrayed him.

Trust should exist before the relationship evolves into a committed one. However, if a woman is not sure who she is, she might decide to adapt to someone else's idea of who she is. She may become the person her husband prefers to ensure that she will be loved and accepted. Ironically, she does this for love, but the love she is receiving is not for her, for her true self, but for her fabricated self. She is deceiving him and herself. Strangely then, when she finally grows up and she has the courage to be herself, she will blame her partner for not understanding her and not loving her for who she is. She will forget that she never showed him her true self. To be fair to the husbands, it is not their fault that their wives choose to be someone else in the relationship.

Cyrus started very early in our marriage to use the culture difference as justification for something I would disapprove of. He realized that comments like "You cannot understand because you are not Persian," put the blame on me, or so I felt. It was my fault that I could not share his views. He knew that my request to have him stay with me instead of going to New York was a valid one. He knew that his presence and help after the birth of our child was important, but he was unable to stand up for what was important to me. There were many occurrences which made me think I was in the wrong relationship, but the hope that things would change always accompanied me. I always expected him to make things right.

It never occurred to me that I had a responsibility to voice my views and to be firm about what I wanted. I thought that if he loved me, he should know what I need, without being told. I feel this is the worst thing women do to men. In general, we women have a misconception that men should be as intuitive as we are and should know what we think and what we want. I am sure that on rare occasions this happens, but in the majority of instances, men cannot read minds; they need to be told what we think. Cyrus must have realized early on how he could manipulate me, but it was also my fault that I did not stand up for myself. I made it easy for him to control me. His cultural right to be the leader in the relationship coupled with my inability to stand up for myself made it very easy for him to take total control of my life.

If you cannot freely express your needs and wants regardless if they meet the approval and acceptance of your partner, it is a sign that you are losing yourself in the relationship. This does not necessarily happen only between people of different cultures, it can also happen if you feel intimidated by the strong personality of your partner or by virtue of some other weakness you may have in your personality.

I believe women have a primary need to understand finances and to know what is real and what is not. When a fundamental need or want cannot be expressed in the relationship, trust cannot be achieved. There may be cultural taboos that create barriers to trust, but unless you have the freedom to ask questions and understand the profound differences that might divide you, you risk building up resentments - which eventually bring you to separation. More important, if you give up your right to express yourself and give a voice to your needs and wants, you will not be able to use your inherent wisdom.

Chapter 5
Two: Becoming Financially Dependent

At the beginning of our marriage, I was the breadwinner. Then, I became totally dependent on Cyrus for about sixteen months after the birth of our first child. I returned to work for the next four years, and things were getting back to normal. We divided the expenses, and there was some balance. I felt good about regaining my independence and pride in what I was doing in my job. I was an investigator of fraud for the federal government and sure to climb the professional ladder.

After our decision to have a second child, I became dependent again. I thought that Cyrus would have been fair, so while I was busy with the new baby and my first son, I gratefully gave him total control of the finances. I thought it would be temporary. He liked the role of the breadwinner, the man in the family—the role so familiar to his cultural background. It wasn't long before I realized I had made a big mistake. It was very difficult to regain control over managing anything in the house. He allowed me full control only of the children when they were young.

When my second child started kindergarten, with my children and my husband out of the house from 8:20 a.m. to 4:00 p.m., I believed I could pursue a career of my own and fulfill my intellectual needs. Being a mother was emotionally fulfilling and I was definitely very busy. Many women are happy and satisfied with this role, and I am happy for them, but I personally felt that something was missing. I was not stimulated enough intellectually. I also knew I had something more to offer to society. I volunteered in the hospital, and I taught few classes as a substitute and heritage teacher, but it was not enough. My mind was crying for something more challenging.

I approached Cyrus with the proposal that I return to work, maybe to my career with the federal government as an investigator of fraud or maybe to find a new career. His answer was always a threat. "If you go to work, we will divorce. You know my working hours; we would never be able to see each other. I make enough money for both of us," he would say, "and you should be happy to be a mother and a wife. Other women would give an eye to be in your place. Why do you want to work anyway?" He would also say, "The money you will make will not even pay for the housekeeper and the expenses of the car or the baby sitter. By the time you pay the taxes, you are working for nothing. If you can't make at least $100,000 per year, it is not worthwhile."

No amount of money I could have earned would have been of any value to him. He dismissed all the other reasons for my wanting to work. He believed that money was power and that individual prestige was measured by one's pocketbook or occupation. Engineers and doctors are the only two professions respected in his culture. Every Iranian parent aspires to have their children become doctors or engineers. Being a lawyer is not as good unless you are a prominent one, but you can be a lousy doctor or engineer and that doesn't matter because you have the prestigious title. I could never understand that, and it was a common point of conflict between Cyrus and me.

This conversation often occurred at the dinner table, as he wanted our children to know what he thought about the issue. He wanted his children to become a doctor or an engineer, nothing else. I would contradict him, saying it doesn't really matter which profession the children choose as long as they get a university education. I wanted my children to choose the careers they wanted, and I wanted them to be happy and self-assured. Our children would tell him that they did not want to become doctors or engineers. Their comments were received with strong disapproval, as if they were disobedient to his grand plan.

The meaning of success was a common point of conflict between us. I believe that the loss of wealth his family suffered due to his father's gambling left large scars on his fragile sense of worth. Cyrus was a man of contradiction as well. His opinions about personal worth didn't stop him from being very generous with people in need. He helped many people: family, friends, and strangers. He had an incredible respect for the elderly. While servicing his clients, I learned of his many acts of kindness and charity.

I believe that his decision to disregard my needs was motivated by his fear of losing his power in the relationship as the breadwinner. He was afraid that if I became financially independent, I would not need him and I would leave him. He did not want to lose my complete dedication, morning and night, to his needs. He was afraid to disrupt the harmony and the balance in our family. For him, traditional roles were well defined in the context of the family. He had not witnessed the social revolution of the 60s and 70s in his own country.

In the early 60s, Iranian law regarded women in the same class as minors, criminals, and the insane. They could not vote or stand for public office. They were not allowed guardianship of their own children, could not work or marry without permission from their male benefactors, could be divorced at any moment by the utterance of a simple sentence from their husband, or could be faced with the presence of a second, third, or fourth wife in their home. Women had no legal, financial, or emotional recourse. If their husband died, they still could not become guardians of their children. They could not transfer their citizenship to their children; indeed, their citizenship was in jeopardy if they married a non-Iranian. They inherited from their father's estate only half of what their brothers received. They inherited one-fourth of a husband's estate when there were no children and one-eighth if there were children.

The late 60s and 70s brought some progressive legislation such as the Family Protection Law, which abolished extra-judicial divorce, greatly limited polygyny, and established special family courts. During the Shah's reign, women acquired the right to vote and to be considered a legal entity equal to men.

In the west, the 60s and 70s brought different types of revolution: the women's revolution and a societal revolution. It was a time when men were confused about their role in society and in relationships. Men had to adapt to a different definition of manhood. They weren't necessarily the sole provider or decision maker in the family. Sexual roles were redefined, and women were freer to express themselves sexually, which men did not expect or readily accepted.

I was struggling to be heard and to be considered knowledgeable in business matters, so I presented a business proposal to Cyrus. Yes, I tried to keep hope alive. I loved to design clothing, and together with a friend designed a line. We approached manufacturers in Florence and Prato, the heart of clothing manufacturers and materials in Italy. We made samples and had success with some Canadian stores, but we needed financial support to produce the line. Cyrus let me go to Italy to explore this business adventure, and he seemed supportive at the beginning, but when I asked for his financial support, he refused.

I think he never believed I was capable of succeeding in the venture, and he thought he would let me play with the idea just for me to have some fun. He expected me to fail eventually, proving his point that I was not capable of getting into business, and that I should accept my role in the home. I had no money in my account except the money he was giving me at the beginning of each month. At the end of the month, I had very little left. I had no access to his bank accounts, so I was at his mercy. I did not proceed with the project. My friend continued with her creations and business; she now owns a very successful boutique.

A few months later, Cyrus invested a large amount of money in a manufacturing company owned by a client of his who wanted to separate from his partner. Cyrus entered into partnership with this gentleman, and because he could not have a business while he was an insurance agent, he listed me as the owner and a silent partner of the company. Ironically, it was a clothing manufacturing company. We lost a lot of money, and the only consolation was that for many years we provided work for fifteen to twenty people. My sense of self-worth plunged. I felt very bad in the position he had put me into, with a partner I did not know, and with no power whatsoever. I felt helpless, used, like a puppet, and excluded from the financial decision making of the family.

Society in general and men in particular wrongly believed that women were not capable of making good financial decisions, even if statistics proved them wrong. Women have traditionally worked miracles in managing households with limited resources. Now, in the western world, more successful small businesses are managed and owned by women. Less than a century has passed since women have been recognized as full participants of society, and women today are a strong force in the economy of many nations. Still, there is much work to be done to achieve equality. But, give us enough time and opportunities, and we will be there. I am pleased to say that today in 2012 we have twenty women heads of state in the world, not including queens and princesses. Encouragingly, some third world countries where women still fight for equality have elected women as heads of state.

In retrospect, I don't know if insisting on working outside the home would have changed Cyrus's mind. I remember feeling hopeless when we argued, and he made me feel guilty about having aspirations beyond my role as a mom and a wife. It was like he felt I was not grateful for his hard work. I could remember when I also felt that way. When I was a young adult, my parents continuously complained about how much money they were spending for us children and told us we should always be grateful and not ask for more. I always felt I owed them something and that we were a great burden to them. Because of this, I developed a need to never be a burden to anybody and to be independent, hence my running away and making a life of my own away from home.

Then, with Cyrus, I had someone telling me, "You don't need to work and be independent," but at the same time making me feel, as my parents did, that I should be appreciative of what he offered. I take responsibility for not having argued and debated the issue about working outside the home. Still, I believe working outside the home would have contributed to my self-esteem and allowed me to regain the financial independence I craved so much. I decided to return to school instead. I planned to postpone my request and build more opportunities for when I would eventually go back to work. I attended the university and earned a couple of degrees in psychology.

Seven Signs That You Are Losing Yourself in a Relationship

Do you feel that every time you decide to do something or organize something, your partner comes up with another idea, which he will then try to push as the better one? After trying many times to get your idea taken into consideration, do you give up because he always seems to win, or for whatever reason, you let him win? Think about why you give up. Are you motivated by fear? If the issue is about choosing a movie or a holiday destination, do you fear he will not come with you and therefore spoil the family time? Is the price of a lousy holiday or going to a movie alone too high for a future of compromise and better relationships? What other fears do you have?

How often do you felt devalued, ignored, or have your suggestions regarded as stupid, impossible, or crazy? Do you ever feel invisible? No matter how many times you try to propose an idea or project, do you find yourself ignored or ridiculed? Or worse, does your spouse later propose the same ideas as his own? Do you feel he is not listening to you? Is he so convinced that you can't have a good idea or he has a better one that he doesn't pay attention when you express yours?

Sometimes, we don't assert ourselves because we are afraid of the consequences. The fear can be stronger than our needs and desires. It is important to analyze where these fears come from and to minimize them. To do so, it might be helpful to think about the worst thing that can happen if you stand up for your wants and needs. More often than not, we are afraid of the unknown. If we think about the worst thing that can happen, we might find out that it is not that scary at all. This exercise can minimize the fear and can give you some courage to confront your partner with more confidence.

Believe in yourself! Remember that a loving, functional relationship is also a partnership, and in any partnership mutual contribution is required to maintain a balance. I hope that you will find the courage to fight for your needs. I want you to think about the times you have approached your spouse with your needs and desires and you have felt rejected. When I talk about needs, I mean any need, from sexual needs to simple needs such as what you prefer to eat on a particular day or the movie you want to see.

Chapter 6
Three: Living in Fear and Walking on Eggshells

In my young life, I received physical and verbal abuse from my parents, and I still have the scars. I can remember the intensity of the pain, the feeling of impotence, and the feeling that I must be a bad girl if even my parents couldn't love me. I felt a sense of isolation and injustice, and that the whole world was against me. I had no place to go, and no confidence with which to react to the injustice. There is not much difference between physical abuse and verbal abuse except the time it takes to feel the consequences of it.

Throughout our relationship, I fell in and out of love with my spouse. At times he was sweet, loving, funny, warm, and romantic. As intense as these expressions were, so were the moments of rage, impatience, and threats. He never hurt me physically. He was a very gentle man dealing with his demons. The unpredictability of his moods put me always on alert and made me walk on eggshells. I often asked myself, "Will it be okay today to tell him something, or should I wait until tomorrow?" On one day, everything was fine and I felt comfortable and safe to talk to him about some sensitive issue. On another day, the same subject would become a point of argument. I was confused. I thought it must be me: maybe my approach was wrong, maybe my tone of voice was wrong, maybe I chose the wrong moment.

It was impossible to have a difference of opinion. Early in our relationship, we fought about something every day. Our lack of communication, coupled by cultural differences, caused many conflicts. He told me once to please not contradict him when he talked, even if I disagreed with him. Remembering my mother's wedding-day advice, "The stronger one is the first one to give up in an argument," I gave it a shot. I stopped contradicting him and noticed that, due to my efforts, our arguments diminished. For the longest time, I thought I had made the right choice. What was I doing, though? I was losing my voice in our marriage, and our relationship was losing its balance and spontaneity.

So many times, I felt threatened by Cyrus's tone of voice. When he was losing an argument, he would soon raise his voice. That was enough for me to relive the same emotions I felt as a child regarding the incident with my father when I was seven or when my mother was about to beat me for displeasing her. To this day, I feel fear any time anybody's voice raises. My fear response is diminishing, and I have learned to deal with it, but I still experience that uncomfortable feeling every time somebody uses an irate tone of voice.

Cyrus used his intimidating voice not only with me but also with his children. He never touched them physically, but they knew he was very serious about his rules, and they would not challenge him. They did not like to bring their friends home because their friends felt intimidated by him. He had never used words to cause their friends' feelings. It was something else about him, his body language and his look: Cyrus's look. He could look people straight in the eyes in a way that made them feel he could see through them.

He loved his children dearly, but he felt he had to seem severe to prevent them from going astray. He really was a pussycat who enjoyed being a wolf from time to time. I disagreed with his tactic, and to compensate, I was always extra cautious not to intimidate my children's friends. I wanted my home to be seen by my children and their friends as a welcoming home and a place where they could feel comfortable. I believed that if you provided such an environment for your children and their friends, you would have the opportunity to monitor their lives in a non-threatening, noninvasive manner.

Cyrus would not allow our children to dress in a certain way. We all know that when children are teenagers, they want to express themselves, and usually they adopt a clothing style worn by the majority of their peers. We argued often about what our children were allowed to wear. I allowed my son to dress in the special, admittedly weird, clothing of the eighties -ruffled shirts and all, and made sure Cyrus never saw him wearing those clothes. I wanted to be what my mother never was., the contrasting and protective counterpart , the voice of reason and balance - I did not know at the time if it would have been accepted by my children the way it was intended. Luckily my children assure me know that it did. I felt guilty, and found myself lie to him. I also knew that if the rules were too strict or irrational, the children would certainly break them, and I was more afraid that they would break some rules that might have put them in danger. Most of the time, I felt like a third child in the family, and as such I felt that under the circumstances, I had to break the unfair rules myself. What I considered to be his irrationality and unpredictability forced me to lie, to walk on eggshells, and to feel so guilty about it.

Cyrus could be very generous with his money. He spent a lot for what he believed was important: private schools for our children, vacations, and decorating the home, but the money was always spent only on what he believed we needed, hence the control. He had a bad habit of reminding me how much he was spending for all the benefits we enjoyed. Because I was often criticized about spending too much money, many times I found myself coming home with shopping bags when I was sure he would not see me. I would go straight to the bedroom and hide what I had just purchased. I was longing for the time when I could happily buy a dress and show it to him expecting a compliment about my choice. It never happened. So, I preferred to lie and say that I got it in Italy as a present from my family. I learned how to walk on eggshells.

When I look back on this period of time and try to find reasons for Cyrus's behavior, I can't help thinking about an episode that occurred at our kitchen table one Sunday morning during our brunch. We were ready to start our meal. My first child, then fourteen or fifteen, came last to the table. He said good morning, and as soon as he sat down something very unusual happened. Cyrus started speaking in Farsi and gave our son a slap on the face. Cyrus had never touched our children under any circumstances. It was so out of character and so scary. The children were shocked, and I was ready to take his eyes out. He soon apologized and then asked my son who gave him the right to shave his moustache.

We were all confused. At that moment, I realized that he had shaved the soft fuzzy hair on his upper lip. I thought it was cute before, but regarded it as a mature thing that he decided to shave it. I was fine with it, but Cyrus's reaction was, to say the least, weird. Here again, our cultural differences played a big role. Apparently, in Iran shaving the moustache for the first time is a big deal. The boy must ask permission many times and be refused a few times until the father consents. Then, the father will do it for the son. We were oblivious of this tradition, and Cyrus's reaction was so strong that we did not know what to do. We did not know what other traditions we should have known about before our actions would cause similar reactions.

Cyrus's expectations about his role as the patriarch had been violated by the customs in the west. In his culture, as long as you live with your parents, you must ask permission about everything. In the west, children are encouraged to make decisions about their personal and intimate issues on their own. My son thought his father would accept him with a pat on the shoulder and say something nice about becoming a man. What he got instead was quite different. Cyrus apologized again for his reaction after he had a moment to reflect, and we all understood and forgave him. To this day, we still remember the episode and laugh about it, but at the time it was serious. It was another incident that reminded Cyrus of the differences between us, and his inability to have it both ways. He saw the value of having the family in the west and all the opportunities that it brought, but he had to be reminded that it came at a cost -which perhaps he was not ready to pay.

It was also the time of the revolution in Iran. Seeing every day the destruction caused in his country by the west, and believing the U.S. had something to do with the downfall of the Shah, he must have been in serious conflict about his values, priorities, and roles in life. It was during this period that he had the affair with the Persian woman. It must have been his need to have an ally, someone from a similar background who could understand his inner feelings, his internal language, and the pain he was feeling over losing his homeland. I have rationalized and forgiven, but the damage remains.

At times, when the discussion was heated and he could not win the argument, he reverted to his native language, saying things I could not understand. Then, he would get upset with me because I could not understand his language. I would tell him that he knew enough English to verbalize what he wanted to say, but he would retort that it was more accurate if said in Farsi. He excluded me totally from what he felt and what he wanted to communicate because he knew we had opposite ideas and values.

Mi escludeva totalmente da quello che pensava, sentiva o voleva comunicare. Era una sensazione sconcertante e sapeva anche che le nostre idee e valori erano diversi.

How did you feel when you tried to read that sentence? If you can read Italian, you had no problem. The majority of you must have felt a little as I did when I was shut off from his thoughts and feelings. When we can't hear the other person and communication shuts down, our minds become active. When we don't know what our partner thinks, our minds create disconnection.

Unable to talk openly about issues, I believed that Cyrus did not respect my opinion. Secrecy became part of nearly everything I did. I didn't tell him how much I spent for a dress, or where the children were, or what clothing they wore. My inherent wisdom had not died, and I decided to bring up my children the way I wanted to, even if it was opposite to his idea of how to raise them. I believed that his way was damaging to them, and I found myself giving our children freedoms he would not agree to, like wearing trendy clothing.

He did not give the children freedom to express themselves and find out who they were. He had decided that his children had to become doctors or engineers. Neither of them wanted to, but that did not matter. I was aware that I was openly contradicting him, but I remembered what happened when I was a child and teenager. My parents forbade me everything. I learned that it is dangerous for parents to be extreme and unfair, as children will rebel. In order to feel sane, the only solution for me was to break as many rules as I could. I did not want our children to have the same experience. We all walked on eggshells. The children had to have a release valve. I suppose I was it. I had to protect my children.

When we are often afraid of our partners' reactions, something terrible happens to the relationship. We lose some of the most crucial tools of communication: spontaneity and truth. We find ourselves selecting what we want to share with our partner, when we share it, and whether we even want to share it. When we must talk to him about something important, we try to discover first what his mood is, find the exact time when we can talk to him, and even if we are careful about choosing the right time, more times than not it is the wrong time. We seem to always walk on eggshells.

When you walk on eggshells, you live a secret life. This is a sign you are losing yourself. If you have reached the third sign, you are living a life of fear, and you have stress hormones flowing through your veins. It is like someone is chasing you, and your stress hormones are increasing. This leads to illness. It is easy for women who do not meet their own needs, who do not have a voice, who go against their own wisdom, and who act in secrecy to become ill and prone to accidents.

Not being able to share in the decision-making may, at some point, create resentments and the destruction of your relationship. You are on a collision course. If you are reading this book, if it makes sense to you, and if you feel that you are shutting down your inherent wisdom, this third sign is a serious one that needs your prompt attention. If you are walking on eggshells, do you want your children to witness this and to be exposed to this dynamic between you and your partner? Even if you give in to his rules, your children will know that you have given in. What a bad example you are giving to your children!

Be honest, how often do you hide from your partner what you bought? How many times do you keep secret some naughty behavior of your children for fear that your partner will be too severe with their punishment? And how often have you been afraid to approach your spouse because you thought he was in a bad mood? How often have you convinced yourself that your request, which a minute ago felt important, suddenly became unimportant?

I hope that if you read about my experiences and recognize yourself in my story, you will find the courage to accept reality and talk about it with a trusted friend or someone who can help you discover the best way to approach these issues with your partner. Not everybody benefits from or needs psychotherapy. The compassionate and loving ear of a friend can also work wonders.

Chapter 7

Four: Giving Up Your Personal Values

If you come from different cultures, you come with certain inherent values. You bring those values into your relationships. I was an Italian woman and Cyrus was an Iranian man. Italy had been going through a social evolution since the 50s. All of Europe and North America went through a social revolution in the 60s. Women's rights were at the forefront of social changes in the western world, and I was enchanted by the affect women were having on the North American social fiber.

I came to Toronto from Italy, where as students we organized demonstrations about anything that was going on in the world. Mostly, it was a good excuse to skip school and make noise. We disrupted traffic, received swear words from drivers, and we all thought we made an impact. We really didn't; there was no media coverage and no change in the system. We had no voice in a country thousands of years old with rules and laws older than Methuselah.

The first demonstration in Toronto that I participated in was about women's rights. We were no more than 200 people versus a group of thousands in Italy. I was shocked to see the story on the first page of the main Toronto newspaper the next morning. I decided then that Canada was going to be my country. Cyrus, on the other hand, was a very conservative man who adopted the external appearance of Europeans, but in his heart, he was a Persian man with the strong sense of responsibility and privilege inherent in his patriarchal society.

Regarding women's rights, we could not have been further apart in our values. His idea of womanhood was contrary to mine. However, his actions toward me at the beginning of our relationship did not reflect his true values. He talked and acted like a modern western man. It wasn't until few years later, after he was successful in his career and after he acquired a certain social status that he felt more confident about expressing himself and his true values came to light.

He usually talked about the role of women in the family. He had no problem with women participating fully in the community in every aspect, except in the family. In the family, the man had to be the decision maker, especially about the finances. His attitudes about family life and gender roles became stronger and more conservative with the arrival of his family from Iran during the Iranian revolution. I suppose that as he was reminded of his cultural values and influenced by his family, he felt stronger in opposing my views. He started talking more about the loose morals of women in the west versus the purity of women in Iran.

I was offended, being a woman of the west myself. I resented the fact that he would express these views in front of our children, telling them that they should marry a virgin. I thought that was absurd, and it was the subject of heated discussions between us. What happened to the suave man I met years before who believed that making love before marriage was not an issue?

Another source of conflict was Cyrus's declarations that western girls could not be trusted and they were not pure because they do not remain virgins before marriage. It hurt me when he said this, especially in front of my children who were westerners and had a western mother. He always followed those statements with, "except your mother." This infuriated me, because I knew he did not mean it. Sometimes, I believed he said it on purpose to make me feel that I wasn't that great and that he was doing me a favor by accepting me even though I was damaged goods.

Many times, the subject of marriage in his culture or mine came up. He was a Shia Muslim and he defended the fact that his religion allowed temporary marriages while I was appalled by it. I called it - legalized prostitution. He claimed that temporary marriages protected the wife and society from sickness. His reasoning was that if a married man was entered into a temporary marriage with a virgin girl whom he was sure did not have any sexually transmitted disease - he could not pass any disease to his wife. According to Cyrus, in the west married men have sex with prostitutes or other women who are, of course, promiscuous and therefore spread sexually transmitted disease.

It made me furious that he could not see the cruelty of temporary marriage. The women in temporary marriages were always poor women, as young as nine years old, who either gave themselves or were given by their parents to all types of men, young and old, who could afford to pay for them. The women were paid a sum of money for their services. They were paid after the last sexual encounter, but they had to wait four months to make sure they were not pregnant. If they were, the men supported the child. Parents literally sold their daughters to make money. To me, that is prostitution of the worst kind. Those poor women had no chance to marry anybody else, as they had lost that most precious thing that Iranian men looked for in a potential wife, their virginity. We could not agree on these issues at all.

When Cyrus was growing up in Iran, multiple wives were allowed. Even his father's twin sister was one of four wives. Cyrus said it was not something he would do, but defended the practice as being good for women, who outnumbered men, because the women could have a man to take care of them and they could become mothers. His views were so contrary to what I, or any western woman, would accept as ideology. Still, I did not see his beliefs as a possible threat to our union. He declared he would not do it and I interpreted his comment as a criticism of the practice. It was much later in our relationship, after the reunion with his family and culture that he started to defend and justified the practice.

My husband's idea of success was different from mine. I liked the good life, and I appreciated the lifestyle I was living, but sometimes when I was looking at the $40,000 ring on my finger, it felt like a ball and chain. During our relationship, we tried not to talk about politics and religion; they were two subjects we knew we would argue about. I was always in search of the meaning of our existence and trying to open my mind to different philosophies or religions. Cyrus had no interest in exploring that way. I never saw him read a book.

Cyrus was changing before my eyes. During the time of the Iranian revolution, he was very angry at the west, especially the U.S. He became angry seeing everything the Shah had built being destroyed by the Mullah. Cyrus supported everything the Shah dreamed about for his native country. We spent every day watching news on TV; it was ever present on every television in the house. We did not miss any information coming from Iran. Cyrus could not believe what was happening to the people in the streets of Iran. "Where do they come from?" he would ask. "I have never seen these people in Iran. The veil was abolished in the 30s; it was tolerated only in remote villages." He was shocked and angry that modern Iranian people were portrayed to the world as a bunch of Bedouins.

Cyrus's entire family had to escape from Iran under dangerous circumstances. Some had to cross the border into Turkey under the bellies of donkeys to hide from guards. He had every right to be angry and sad, but he had no right to put hatred in the minds of our children. Iranians opposing the ousting of the Shah were all in agreement about their hatred toward the west. It was this negative attitude that Cyrus wanted to convey to our children, and I was continually opposing him. It became a battle of western versus mid-eastern moral values, and it encompassed loyalty to country and loyalty to our people.

We had agreed to raise our children with a strong bond to the country of their birth, yet they were hearing so much negativity toward the west— so many contradictions. Due to the dark color of their skin, our children were called offensive names and because of their connection to Iran, they were threatened as well. It was a dreadful time in history, especially in our family's history. I fought hard to achieve some balance, but daily they were seeing conflicts outside their home, and inside as well. I had to stop fighting with Cyrus because I was worried about my children.

Fearful of a possible break up, I did something awful, which I regret to this day. I conformed even more to Cyrus's image of a wife. "If you were Persian, you would understand," he would often say. I could not accept the teaching of hate, but I was fearful of losing my family, so I became the best Persian wife one could be without being Persian. I cooked Persian food, I learned Farsi, and I associated primarily with Persians.

When you accept the first sign, the second sign, and the third sign, it is likely that you are giving up your personal values.

In a bicultural relationship, we may tend to embrace the other culture for various reasons, including our need for acceptance, love, or comfort. Sometimes, we do it out of fear. In order to be accepted by Cyrus, I had to be as Persian as possible. He was fascinated by foreign girls, but he also wanted someone who could understand him, his culture, his music, and his language. He wanted someone who could be everything a Persian girl could be without actually being Persian. I didn't understand it, but I became as close to a Persian girl as I could. I learned the language and cooked the food, but apparently I wasn't submissive enough.

I wanted to be accepted by his whole family and by the Persian society in Canada. Most of all, I wanted Cyrus to be proud of me, and he was. I believe, though, he was most proud of the fact that he had finally succeeded in changing me into a nice Persian girl. In his mind, he had won. At that same time, he started an affair with the young Persian girl, a friend of the family. I believe she satisfied his need to feel understood about the pain regarding the demise of his native land and to be consoled the way that only a person going through the same pain could do. This included talking bad about who they thought permitted the destruction of their country: the Americans and the west.

If you are in a relationship in which the man believes that the woman must be virgin when they marry, and the woman does not share the same belief, shame enters into play. Such a difference in beliefs changes the dynamics in the relationship. You cannot be in a healthy relationship if you feel shame about who you are or what you believe in. In your most precious relationship your partner, if you cannot be yourself, if you cannot express what you like, if you cannot state what your values are and live by them without feeling judged and shamed, then you are in the wrong relationship.

Do you feel pressured to conform and adhere to your spouse's ideas? Do you feel threatened if things are not done the way he wants? Do you fear that there would be no harmony in the family, or worse, that he might leave you if you express yourself? It might start with little things like the type of food he wants you to cook, the frequency with which you visit your in-laws, or the subtle isolation from your friends. It progresses with the dislike of the clothing you wear or your new haircut.

After a while when you realize that you have given up your voice, you also realize that you have given up your soul. Your personal values are at the base of who you are and what inspires you. Think back before you were in your relationship. Your values were to be honest and loving and to do 'good' in the world. If you are not able to voice your opinion or your disapproval of your spouse's conduct, you are in conflict with yourself and your values, which can prevent you from accessing your soul.

Do you realize you have different views, yet instead of confronting him and coming to a compromise do you give up and comply with his demands? Are you, even if slightly, afraid of him and his reactions? Please learn from my mistakes. You are giving away a part of yourself to someone who will not cherish it but will use it against you. *He fell in love with who you were. As you change, even if it is to who he wants you to be, you are in his eyes a different person. If can manipulate you, he loses respect for you.* Don't allow this to happen. Stand firm in your beliefs. Always remember, the children are watching, and if not for the children—you might not have children—what about you, your soul, your survival?

Chapter 8
Five: Afraid to Confront a Breach in Trust

About six years before Cyrus's death, I had survived the revolution of Iran. Little did I know, I was about to encounter the most difficult upheaval in my life: I had to fight for the survival of my marriage. I was preoccupied with the university and our children; I did not notice the danger around me.

One of the strongest bonds I thought I had with my spouse was our equally intense commitment to our family unity and our children. We were very sure of each other's commitment to both. I never doubted Cyrus's commitment and fidelity. I believed him to be honorable, moral, and devoted to our family. His moral social persona was so important to him that I never thought he would jeopardize it with an affair. He was very romantic and continuously assured me with words of his love for me. He often talked about his friends being unfaithful and criticized them for their actions. "There is nothing better than making love with your wife," he would comment after our lovemaking. I was so happy to hear his words. I felt special and lucky.

My life was very good at that time. I was going to school and learning things I always wanted to learn. My mind was satisfied, and our social life was full. We traveled a lot, enjoyed beautiful things, and I knew I was living a privileged life. My dependence on Cyrus still bothered me, though. His complaints about my spending were irrational, and we continued to have conflicts. I was ready to confront him again with the issue of my returning to work, and this time I was determined to win the argument.

His response was the same; there was no change in his determination to keep me dependent on him. My education might have made him a bit insecure about my intentions to stay in the marriage. It was at that time that Cyrus bought me the beautiful $40,000 diamond ring. I chose the diamond and designed the setting. It was the first time I had the privilege of choosing my gift. Before then, he had never given me a gift I chose, but rather what he liked—Persian jewelry of course. I thought I had arrived, so I attributed a much deeper value to the diamond ring than it actually had. For Cyrus, the ring was his announcement to the world that he had arrived and that he had regained the dignity he lost when his family became poor due to his father's gambling.

I must admit that the financial security was appealing and reassuring. I knew I never had to worry about the future because Cyrus's career was booming. I became too sure about it, and I even felt entitled to it. Most of the people we frequented were wealthy, and I became accustomed to a certain lifestyle. I liked things as they were. Maybe my greed blinded me as much as my fear. I did not notice anything negative around me. Things were happening, though, that I could not define: I knew that something was threatening our family.

We started getting strange phone calls at unusual times. Cyrus's comment was, "Somebody is trying to put some problem between us." I decided to accept his explanation. Cyrus left the house every night at 7:00 p.m. and came back about 11:00 p.m., sometimes at 12:00 a.m. He would tell stories about the traffic or the obstacles causing him to be late, and I would accept his explanations. I never doubted him. I had no reason to doubt him. Except for the phone calls, our life as a couple was normal. Sex was good and frequent, and words of love were exchanged. I don't know to this day if he was able to love me while he loved someone else or if it was all a charade.

I was still busy with my university studies, and my life seemed to be normal until one day when Cyrus brought up the subject of blackmail. He talked about it too much, and I realized he was being blackmailed. I thought it was about business matters. He denied it; he said it was just a thought. A week later, I decided to open the subject of blackmail at the dinner table. I directed my comments to Cyrus and to the children. I told them that if someone should ever blackmail them, they must tell their family. "Never fall into the trap, because there is nothing, and I mean nothing, that you cannot tell your family and be forgiven," I told them.

A couple of days later, I was making a special Persian marmalade with quince apples. I was very proud to show him that I could make the marmalade just like his sister. I saw the lights of his car approaching the house, and I went to the front door to greet him with a kiss as usual, when I saw her standing next to him. They said hello, and he didn't kiss me. I immediately knew. This Persian girl he so strongly wanted me to befriend and mentor, the poor young mother of two children left by her husband, stood in front of me in my house, and she was not there for a visit.

The life was sucked out of my soul. I started to feel light-headed, but I put a courageous smile on my face and I gestured to come into the living room, pretending that I did not understand. They both sat down. She informed me that they had been having an affair for the past four years and that he promised her he would divorce me and would marry her. Now he wanted to end their relationship, and she felt she was entitled to compensation. I was shocked and thought it must be a Muslim custom that when you leave your concubine you should pay her, but I knew I was in Canada and this did not apply. She wanted $300,000. I informed her that I knew of their affair, that the moment she opened her mouth she lost the $300,000, and I asked her to leave my home.

Everything I had suspected, consciously and through my nightmares, became reality. I did not want to confront it. My life was not my life anymore. I felt I was a character in a puppet show with no control whatsoever. I had ignored many hints about Cyrus's infidelity. Now I had to confront the truth about their affair, and that my man, the one I loved, the one I believed had such high moral standards and whom I trusted with all my might was a fake. I didn't know which truth was more difficult or painful to confront: his breach of trust, the realization that I could be so easily fooled, or that my feelings held no value for him.

In retrospect, I can think about many hints I ignored. They all came to mind after the revelation, but it was my fear that did not let me confront them when there might have been a chance to prevent the mess we found ourselves in. What does it mean to trust another person? Is there a level of trust? Is there blind trust? Conscious trust? After my experiences, I do not advocate for blind trust.

When something major happens, when a breach of trust occurs, we react with shock because we had not allowed ourselves any awareness that signs were there before—signs about the event, but also about the character of the individual who caused the breach of trust. We ignored the little signs along the way, because accepting the possibility of what they might mean was too painful. It is important to recognize and deal with the small breaches that happen on a regular basis.

I had tried to ignore Cyrus's explicit expressions of disapproval about me. I was not a Persian girl. I was perfect in many ways, except that I was short and not Persian. I was bothered by these comments. I retorted that when someone loves another person, it does not matter where that person comes from. Love conquers all. I was naive and idealistic. I believed that love does not see physical shortcomings or citizenship. Love is just love. It is there or not, period. I did not believe, or I did not want to believe, that he really believed what he was saying—a very common mistake when we project into our man attributes we would like our man to have. I heard him, but I had not listened. How could I accept that the man I loved, spent so many years with, and had two children with, did not like who I was?

We made love and the sex was good. I thought that must mean he loved me and liked me. But then he would make comments, even when I was in good form, exercising and maintaining a good weight. He would say, "Yes you lost weight, but you can never be taller and you cannot change the shape of your body. Your bottom is bigger than your breasts." I never had the confidence or freedom to be seen naked or to make love with the light on. I was ashamed of my body, self-conscious about my unsatisfactory appearance.

In so many subtle ways he told me, "I have lost interest in all the things you offer me that are important. I am now looking for someone who will fit my preferences in women: young, tall, and with proportionate body features and less educated than me." His heart and soul were not working in conjunction with his libido, or his brain for that matter. He was looking for an adventure with his ideal image of what he had missed if he had lived a Persian life. Ironically, even the Persian woman did not satisfy him, and on top of that, she blackmailed him.

I did not get unconditional love from my parents, and I certainly did not get it from my husband, so what is unconditional love? I could see Cyrus's shortcomings, but I could never put them in front of the love I felt for him. So, what is this unconditional love we are all looking for? My idea of unconditional love is to be accepted totally for who I am and to be allowed and encouraged to be the best that I can be. For me, this is love.

Sometimes, we may be confused about the feelings we have for another person. We meet someone, we find them appealing, and we feel a special attraction toward them. We say we are in love, but most of the time our hormones are talking. Most of the time, we look at someone and we like them because they seem to have the qualities we like in a man. If chemistry is also there, we feel so happy that the person has, for example, self-assurance, savoir-faire, intelligence, humor, and good looks that we overlook other important attributes they should have but might not, such as honesty, integrity, finesse of heart. We overlook that they clip the wings of the person they love.

You know that something has changed between you and your spouse, but you cannot pinpoint what it is. You hope for the best, and you ignore the signs. You are afraid that your gut feeling that he is having an affair is true. It is such a terrible thought, you choose instead to put your head in the sand and hope you are wrong. There are so many common signs of infidelity. You likely have read them many times in various magazines, but when it happens to you, you are blinded by fear. If you confront the issue, you must react and act accordingly.

Seven Signs That You Are Losing Yourself in a Relationship

Is this happening to you now? Please listen to your gut feeling; it is probably right. Everything else is just fear. In the course of a relationship, attitudes and feelings can change, and it is inevitable for you to grow as a couple. How much you grow apart, though, determines the future of your relationship. In order for a relationship to survive, even though you don't see eye-to-eye, partners need to bend a little. But if you bend too much, you may lose the balance your relationship needs in order to survive.

Have you ever had a gut feeling about something and dismissed it? Are you doing that now in your current relationship? Can you identify with my story at some level? If you do, please trust your instincts. Act promptly, confront your partner - work it out in whatever way you decide to, but do not ignore what your instinct is telling you. Don't believe him when he tells you that you are crazy. Don't be intimidated by him, but stand your ground and get to the bottom of the situation. I lost myself in my fantasy of what my marriage, my man, and my life was. My fear blinded me for four years.

Chapter 9
Six: Too Apathetic to React to Your Losses

Fear prevailed. I retreated and tried to convince myself that all the issues we fought over were not important when I considered the alternative: divorce and an uncertain future. We had few friends who were not Persian. We had some Italian friends and some friends who were "real Canadian," as we called them, but we socialized with them infrequently. Whenever we had a party, Cyrus did not want to invite them because he thought they wouldn't blend in well with the group.

The problem was that when Persian people got together, they spoke Farsi. It didn't make any difference if you asked them to speak English. They would apologize, say a few words in English, and then revert back to Farsi. I found that very rude. I repeatedly asked Cyrus to respond always in English, so that they would get the message and eventually speak English also. I thought that would solve the problem, but he never agreed to do that. This was about control. In my own home - I was not a full participant. I literally had no voice.

I rationalized every sacrifice I made. I thought, "Who cares if I cook only Persian food? I like the taste of it. If I can't invite our Italian friends,

I can see them on a separate occasion." Of course, many times I also thought, "Why can't the Persians speak English when they are in a multicultural environment? They know the language." I grew tired of having a conflict about this, so I surrendered. Persian it is. I learned a little more Farsi, but I never felt fully accepted. I told myself; "I like the food, I like the people, and it is a small sacrifice to make to please my man." I did not realize that I was isolating myself and that Cyrus was getting less exposure to a diverse social group and eclectic ideas.

He was becoming more Persian. This was not good for him, it was not good for me, and it was definitely not good for our children. Almost all of our social life together was spent with Persian people: his family and his friends. Luckily, I had some kind of escape with my university group. I found my intellectual satisfaction outside our marriage, and gradually Cyrus's opinion did not hold the same value I attributed to it before. I realized that my growth was driving us apart. Any time I wanted to share my newly acquired knowledge, he thought I wanted to show how much he did not know. For a long time, I surrendered.

One of the most dangerous things that can happen to you is if you stop caring about what happens to you, if you become apathetic about what is going on around you. You may reach that point after repeatedly failing in your attempts to be heard. You may think about separation and divorce, but you convince yourself that you cannot do that to your children, and you cannot do it to yourself. So little by little you stop fighting. By doing so, you chip away parts of yourself; you start transforming into someone more acceptable to your spouse but foreign to you.

Little by little, you chip away to the core of your identity, and you find yourself emerging as someone else. You feel like a zombie, but around you everything seems to be in order. Your husband has what he wants, your children have their mom and dad, and you must be grateful that you are not out of the picture. I remember feeling this way many times during our marriage. But after I went to university and I learned more about life, I reached a point where I knew more about myself, too, and I began needing Cyrus's approval less and less.

When you feel you are losing control, you may try to assert yourself as much as possible, to hold your ground—sometimes about silly points that really have no meaning in your life. And then, you may reach a point when you give up. How often do you feel you just don't care anymore? Do you feel that any energy you use on improving your relationship is wasted energy? Do you feel he will never change and so you just better count your losses and move on? Well, I can tell you that there is hope. Circumstances and things and people can change. At the end of his life on this earth and our life together, Cyrus was able to see the gifts life had given him, and our relationship took an interesting turn.

Chapter 10
Seven: Your Personal Growth is Ridiculed

After my apathetic period, I decided to grow intellectually. It had always been, and still is, my goal in life to learn as much as possible during my lifetime. When I learned something new, I wanted to share my new discoveries with the people I knew, especially with my family. I soon realized that Cyrus was not receptive to my sharing. Every time I helped him with the pronunciation of a word or an explanation of it, he would quickly become defensive. "I don't need you to tell me how to say this and that," he would say. "Stop explaining, do you think I am stupid?" I didn't fully understand where that was coming from, but I knew it came from a sense of insecurity.

When I earned my university degree, Cyrus would not come to the graduation ceremony. I was hurt, but I did not make a big deal about it. My apathy still kicked in from time to time. Throughout our years together, I attended university while managing not to have our family life disturbed much, except when exam time came along. I asked my husband and children to be patient with me and to be happy if sometimes we would eat pizza or Swiss Chalet for supper. Our children did not mind much, but Cyrus resented it and couldn't wait until we would return to our normal routine.

While I was attending university, I got involved with COSTI (formerly *Centro Organizzativo Scuole Tecniche Italiane*— literally, Center for Organizational Studies Technical Italian), a great Canadian organization with a holistic view that aspires to meet the needs of newcomers to Canada and their families. COSTI was created sixty years ago by concerned Italian-Canadian citizens and the government of Italy to help Italian newcomers who could not practice their trades without a Canadian equivalent certificate. It eventually disconnected from the Italian government and expanded services to people from all over the world, servicing about 50,000 people per year with a multitude of services (see www.costi.org).

I soon realized that I could provide my services as a counselor, and I started volunteering regularly. I also organized several successful fundraising events. Cyrus rarely participated in them and never donated his money. He left the donations up to me, with my limited resources. I was subsequently elected to the board of directors of COSTI, and I'm still affiliated after twenty-five years. One day, Cyrus confessed to me why he did not come to the fundraisings I organized. He said that if he attended the events, people would think he was successful because of me. I was shocked. I could not understand it.

I thought Cyrus was jealous of my success. He had not had the same opportunity to get an education. There I was, with his help, able to finish at the university. His various comments hurt me very much at the time, as I thought they came from a place of envy: "Now that you have this piece of paper, what do you think you can do with it? Nowadays, it is worth nothing. To have a decent job, you need at least a master's degree." Every time I wanted to take a course to improve myself, I was confronted with comments like, "What do you think you can get with this course? You are becoming a collector of papers that are worth nothing."

Only later did I realize that all his animosity about my education was dictated by his fear that I would understand more about life, his intellectual limitations, and that I would grow so far away from him intellectually that he would lose me. Maybe he also envied the opportunity I had to study. He believed in education, and he helped many people with their school fees. He believed that if given the opportunity, you should stop at nothing less than a PhD.

I didn't think any less of Cyrus for not having a more advanced education. To the contrary, the love I had for him was enhanced by my knowledge of the multiple struggles he had overcome throughout his life. With no opportunities or handouts, he had accomplished a lot. But he missed having an education. He wanted to give others the opportunities he never had to get a higher education.

Cyrus confessed to me that the language I spoke and the subjects I sometimes talked about were foreign to him. My knowledge of the English language was superior to his, especially when I was going to the university. I was excited about learning new things, and I wanted to share it with the whole family. He always interpreted that as my wanting to teach, not share. I suppose my enthusiasm was disarming.

Cyrus confessed to me that many times he felt like an outsider in his own home, and that he pretended he understood our children and me, but most of the time he did not know what we were talking about. He felt excluded, like the children and I were against him. But he never told us. It was a revelation for me, which gave me a different perspective on how he was feeling about his life and the players in it. It was this and many other factors that made me decide to stay in the marriage and work out the many issues that pushed us apart.

We should never be intimidated by anyone to improve our knowledge, to grow spiritually, intellectually, or in any way we like. We should never be afraid to exercise the Godly right to cherish the life we have been given and live it to the fullest.

Cyrus was very sorry about the affair. Most of all, he did not want to hurt our children. I did not want our children to suffer. He pleaded with me to give him another chance. I gave him another chance. Destiny had other plans for Cyrus and me. A couple of years later, while we were still working on our relationship, Cyrus became seriously ill. My life took a 365-degree turn, and I found myself in total control of my family. What would I do with all that control and power? Would thoughts of revenge ever enter my mind, or was the chain broken? What happened next will surprise even the most sophisticated readers.

Part Three

Chapter 11

Bicultural Marital Abyss

After I discovered Cyrus's infidelity with the Persian woman, our relationship took a drastic turn. I felt like I had been in a terrible accident, that I died for a while, and that I was having an out-of-body experience, exactly like some people describe after they have been declared dead. They say the other dimension they experience is so beautiful they do not want to come back into their physical body. In my case, the other dimension was not beautiful. I felt numb for a long while and deprived of the necessary energy to live, to act, to think, and to decide.

I wanted to die, to disappear. But the voices of my children were calling to me with increasing volume. I had to return to reality and confront what was in front of me. I knew that my loving feelings for Cyrus were all gone. I had to reconstruct our relationship. I gave our marriage a second chance. I consciously reconstructed our lives, trying to rebuild the trust that was so violently ripped from my soul. My children pulled me back into life. I reentered my body and my life with Cyrus.

I could not let my children know about the affair. We decided not to live as husband and wife until I decided whether our relationship could survive. I was very angry with Cyrus for bringing this girl to our house on that terrible night to tell me about their affair. Our younger child was sleeping in his room upstairs, but if he wasn't asleep, he could have heard everything going on in the living room. I did not know what they were going to talk about, but Cyrus knew, and he put our child's well-being second: that was too difficult for me to forgive. Maybe mothers have a better sense of protection!

I did not forgive Cyrus for about six months. I thought that if I decided to stay in the relationship, I had to promise myself to never touch the subject again, to move on instead. I thought this would give him the opportunity to regain some dignity and that we could move forward. This was an incredible sacrifice for me: numerous times, I wanted to confront him and ask about details. When? How? How many times you were with her? Why did you feel you needed to betray me? Did you make love to her and then to me on the same day? How could you tell me you loved me when, for years, you were with her? Did you love her? Did you tell her you loved her? How could you do this to us? So many other questions I wanted to ask.

I wanted to physically hurt Cyrus, but I never did. He asked for forgiveness. That night, I left the house, got into my Jaguar, sped out of the driveway, and when I reached the parking lot of my son's school, which was in an isolated area, I screamed until I had no voice left. It was so painful that I wished for death. It took me about thirty minutes to regain my strength. I returned home, went to my bedroom, and started to pack. Cyrus entered the room and asked me what I was doing, physically stopping me from packing. I told him that I could not see his face or hear his voice anymore. He pleaded with me. He reminded me that our sons will ask about me, and he did not know what to answer.

Cyrus pleaded with me to think about our children, to give him another chance, and not to destroy the family. He said he recognized he made a mistake, he never loved her, she had seduced him, he had been weak, he was sorry, and he should have not done what he did. He depicted himself as a victim: he was sorry, she was blackmailing him, and he was convinced that she had been with him only for the money. I wanted so much to believe him that I did.

The dynamic in our relationship changed. I felt then that I had gained more power in our relationship and more respect from him. I now think that it was mostly gratitude for not destroying the family. In my view, he no longer occupied the pedestal I had put him on. Previously, he had convinced me that he was more mature because he was older, that he was more experienced about worldly things, that he was a strong moral man, and that many people admired him and respected him. After his affair was revealed, he started to make favorable comments about my character and personality. I started to see him as a weak, manipulative, naive, vulnerable man who was not so strong after all. During this time, I never blamed myself for what he had done. I had no doubt that under any circumstances, betrayal was unjustified. I developed a more secure sense of myself.

I tried to repair our relationship. I was very hopeful; things were going well under the circumstances. Cyrus tried to reassure me of his fidelity, continually calling me when he worked evenings and giving me the names of people he was with. After a while, I told him he did not need to do that: trust does not require accountability. I started to believe that he had learned something about himself and his priorities, and that earning the love and respect of his children was his priority.

I was sure Cyrus had broken all ties with the Persian woman when, a couple of years later, something arrived in the mail from my university. I thought it was for me; I was the only one affiliated with the university.

When I opened it, I found a receipt of payment for some courses in the name of the Persian woman. When I confronted Cyrus, he swore that there was nothing going on between them, paying for her education was a promise he had made to her, and that it was not honorable for him to break his promise.

How crazy this sounded! I suppose, in Cyrus's mind and according to his tradition, he must have considered her his responsibility: he had a relationship with her similar to a second wife, and therefore he felt he had to take care of her as promised. It did not make sense to me. I thought he must have some attachment to her or he must feel guilty, having lied to her telling her about leaving me and marrying her. She had believed him and waited four years, so when the plan died along with the blackmail, he felt she deserved some compensation.

My antennae were up, and my trust started to diminish. I was scared and confused. I had to make some serious decisions about my life. My trust and love for Cyrus, together with my regenerated sense of security, was on shaky ground. He had assured me that everything was finished with that relationship. To me, that meant never having any kind of contact with that person: that would have made me believe in his good intention to repair our relationship. But again, my needs during this crucial time were not met. Did I need to accept that I was in the wrong relationship? Not only did we have cultural differences, we had different values.

I decided to wait until my younger son finished high school to separate from Cyrus. In the meantime, we fought more, I spoke my mind more, and he did not intimidate me anymore. I started to make plans about what kind of job I might do. I leaned toward a job in psychology or social work. During the summer of the year that my son finished high school, Cyrus got sick with hepatitis B.

I was devastated by Cyrus's death. Everything seemed subliminal. I had so many things to prepare and to take care of that I did not know where to start. The whole family helped beautifully with preparations for the memorial and the funeral. More than 700 people attended the memorial. The place we chose could only contain 700 people, so many were left outside.

On the same day Cyrus's doctors told me that Cyrus had only a few days to live, I received the results of a mammogram that I had after feeling lumps in my breasts: it indicated suspicious cysts and a biopsy was recommended. I had no time to think about me. I had to take the father of my children back to Toronto to die surrounded by the family that loved him. My family came from Italy to be with me and to support me. My brother and my parents left after the memorial service, but my sister remained for a couple of weeks. I could not mourn with so many people around. I waited until I was alone to finally cry.

I soon decided to rebuild my life. My children were watching me. I had to show them I was in control and I could take charge of the family. I had no idea what I was going to do, but I could not let them know that. I entered Cyrus's office and went through his personal files, trying to figure out what I had to do.

During Cyrus's illness, his company helped me to get settled, and seven insurance agents serviced Cyrus's clients. After Cyrus died, I gathered them together in the boardroom. I told them that I was going to take on Cyrus's business, and while I was studying to get my license, they could continue to service his clients: we would split the commission 30/70. While unacceptable to some, a few of them agreed to continue until I could obtain my license. Their support reflected the respect and affection they had toward my husband.

Twenty-five years earlier, I had been a licensed insurance agent, but much had changed since then. Twenty-five years earlier, after I left my bank job due to my wrist injury, I found a job with an insurance company as an insurance agent. I had no car, no connections, and I did not like anything having to do with numbers. But necessity requires adaptation. I was excited about learning new things, and as they promised me during the training, I earned money. I had some success and made some money, but the work was incredibly difficult, and I was not looking forward to doing it again.

I sat in his office viewing the personal files he wanted me to look at in case of his death—files I never saw before, even though I had the keys. While he was traveling, I had plenty of opportunities to see them, but chose not to out of respect. I sat in the chair Cyrus occupied for almost twenty-five years. I touched the arms of the chair, caressing them as I would have caressed his cheeks. Tears ran down my face.

I watered the plants, as I knew he had done numerous times. He loved plants. Then, I went through the files slowly, one by one, looking at the bank statements, income tax returns, and property deeds. And then, one file stood out: a file without a title. My curiosity grew, and when I opened it, I saw photographs of women I knew and others I had never seen, in familiar places around the city or in my house, with poses reflecting familiarity with the person taking the images.

I found many pictures and papers recounting events that occurred, over many years, of relationships not only with the Persian girl I knew about, but with other Persian girls and still others from other cultures. I read through lists and receipts of gifts bought, trips taken, and rents paid: tangible evidence of his many infidelities. My legs started to shake. My head was turning, invaded by multiple images forcing me to confront the ugly truth. Was this what he meant in the hospital when he asked me for forgiveness, when he asked me not to hate him?

My body felt numb for a while, and then my heart started pumping very fast, like I was having a heart attack. I could not breathe properly. An incredible rage came over me. I wanted him in front of me and to hurt him physically. But soon, what came to mind instead was his fragile body, beaten by the lengthy illness, and him looking at me with pleading eyes asking me not to hate him. I did not know what to do. I needed to be angry, but I couldn't be. I had spent so long taking care of his body and his soul; I could not imagine physically hurting such a fragile being. I was still in a protective mode.

But the pain was very strong, and I needed an outlet for my pain; otherwise, I knew I would explode. I could not scream, as I was at his office and people were there. I tried to stop the scream with my hand on my mouth; I pressed it so hard I bruised my face and my gums. I slowly went down to the floor and curled into a fetal position. I stayed there, I don't know how long—maybe one or two hours—telling myself, "This hurts more than his death. I cannot take it. It is not possible. This is not happening to me."

Who was Cyrus? I could not separate him from the fragile image of him that still invaded my memory. I could not be angry with him. I could not wish him pain or death. He had suffered enough and he was already dead. There was no worse punishment for him! What could I do with all this pain and anger about my wasted life? I wanted so much for the pain to stop that I asked God to do something, even if death was the only way to stop the pain. I forgot about my children for a moment, but then my maternal instinct prevailed. This was not the time to think about me. I did not want them to confront another tragedy, and I reminded myself of the role I had accepted to be the rock in their lives. I woke up to reality, and I began to stand up on my wiggly legs even as I sat down on a chair, his chair, the one he touched every day. What irony! This was too much!

I believe that after death, souls travel to a dimension where they are finally able to see everything with clarity and infinite wisdom. Ironically, I turned to Cyrus's pure soul for direction. I believed that he had already served hell in life and that he must have transformed himself into love. I refused to be absorbed by hate. I asked God to please not transform me into a bitter, cynical person and to not take away from me the ability to continue to love deeply and openly. I again reminded myself and repeated to myself over and over again: "Nothing and no one will destroy Vittoria." I thought that if I could get over this, I would be fine in my life.

Looking back, I realize that what was most peculiar about the discovery I made was that Cyrus had introduced me to most of the women he'd had affairs with, asking me to be their friend. In his contorted view of the world and of right and wrong, I think he knew he was doing something wrong towards me, but he thought he could feel less guilty if I knew the women he had affairs with. Trying to make sense of this inexplicable mess, I believe that Cyrus, as a Moslem, felt that if I, his first wife, knew the others, it would seem like an acceptance of other wives in his harem. I don't know why he would want them to be in my life and in his children's lives, but this explanation is what came to my mind. An alternative explanation is that he was so deviant he enjoyed witnessing the relationships between his lovers and me. What is surprising is the women's willingness to befriend me and accept me as their mentor. I believe culture was the culprit here.

It wasn't until late that night that I gained some composure and went home after I was sure my children had gone to bed. I was in a bad physical state with strong a migraine, swollen eyes, and a bruised face. I had reassured Cyrus of my forgiveness as he was dying, but my discovery of the details of his double life was unpredictable and highly disconcerting. I found it very hard that night to feel forgiving. I wondered why he did not destroy everything after we returned to Toronto and before he died. He could have prevented my pain. The only answer I have is that he believed he would survive the transplant.

What need did he have to keep all the documents of his infidelity? Did he consider them as trophies of his charm and his capability to attract all these women? Were they a reminder of great emotions he felt that excluded me? I can't know: without having him available to ask why, I was left with only my imagination. I tried to remember his last words when he used all his will power and came out of a coma to say, "I love my wife; I love my children," but the words were not consoling me, not this time. I carried the pain for a long time. My marriage did not terminate when I decided to leave him prior to his illness or when he died. It terminated when I became aware that his actions stole my past, my history.

There was nothing I was certain of regarding my past with Cyrus. Every emotion I felt in my life had been based on my perception of reality, which now I knew was founded on fantasy. Was I ever really loved by him or by anyone? I was constantly reminded of this vacuum in my life. The only certainty I had was of the joy we both felt about the birth of our children and the wonder of life that children bring. Everything else belonged to a stranger.

Our relationship, as I mentioned earlier, had evolved. He had finally discovered himself and looked at my children and I from a new perspective. I believe he thought that if he could survive his illness, everything would be perfect, and we would be happy in our married life. I had taken on the role of a friend, the best friend he could ever have, who loved him very much for the man he had become. But I could not overlook the man he had been. I knew that even if a miracle occurred, I would never love him as a husband again. It was too late for us, but I promised myself that I would be there for him, the father of my children -loving the man he had become, a dear friend, until his death.

I am very glad I decided not to leave Cyrus before our younger son went to the university. His illness occurred during the summer, just prior to my son's first year of university. If I had left him when I had planned to, he would have been alone when he was diagnosed with hepatitis. If I had left him before he became ill and returned to take care of him, he would not have accepted my help in the same way. He needed to hope and to confront the future with courage and strength. He needed to be sure that better days were ahead in order to fight for his life. I am happy that I was able to do that for him, to let him fight to the end and to support him, even if I did not share his view that everything is possible if you want it and work hard for it.

Six months after Cyrus's death, the Persian woman called me and asked to meet with me. Curious what she wanted to talk to me about, I told her to come to the office. When I asked her why she wanted to meet me, she told me that Cyrus had promised to leave some money for her after his death. According to her, Cyrus left instructions for me to give her a sum of money after he died. I could not believe my ears. Did he really say that to her? I knew that his will did not specify anything about giving her any money, and of course Cyrus had never mentioned anything to me. How could he, when he denied the existence of a relationship between them? She knew that his will had been probated, and if she had been a beneficiary, she would have been called by the lawyers.

She insisted that Cyrus told her he had left some money for me to give to her in the event of his death. If it were not so tragic, it could have been a farce. Was this more cultural mumbo jumbo? I lost my temper. By then, I had read all his secret files. I had seen the receipts for what he spent on her and her family over the course of many years, including plastic surgeries, traveling, and much more. I told her that she had been overpaid for the services she rendered him.

I don't know if this was yet another cultural difference. You see, the first wife in Iran must accept the other women her husband wants to marry. Maybe in Iran, the first wife must also distribute the inheritance to the other wives. I doubt it, and I could not justify her actions. I needed to make sense of it. I asked her to leave. Her last words to me were delivered as a curse or threat, "You have two sons, and you will see what I will do and what will happen to them." After few days, she called the house and left a message for the boys to call her.

I knew then that I had to talk to them. My husband's family knew about this woman, and it wouldn't be long before my children would hear something about their father's infidelity. I decided it was better for them to hear it from me. They knew her very well. As I said before, he would introduce the women to our family. Don't ask me why, I don't get it either.

My children were surprised. Apparently, they never liked her, and my older son said he had some kind of creepy feelings around her. They were upset with Cyrus, but I reminded them repeatedly to make a distinction between the man and their father, and hopefully they did. They realized that his infidelity concerned me as a wife and not them as children. They had to deal with other issues between themselves and their father. I am sure, though, that learning about an unpleasant part of their father's private life must have been very hurtful.

One of the things I was upset about, and maybe my children were also, was that Cyrus never had much time for my children and me. He always complained that he did not have time, and said that if we wanted the lifestyle we had, with Jaguars, diamonds, and private schools, we could not expect to have him around in the evenings, on holidays, or on other occasions. I could not help thinking, and maybe the boys did as well, that supporting another family must have taken a great deal of time—time he could have spent with us. This was very difficult for me to forgive. Cyrus and this woman stole money from my children and me. More importantly, they stole time from us. Later, we realized Cyrus had very little time left. But, as they say, life must go on. I needed to believe in people, and I still believed in love. I had done nothing wrong; wrong was done to me. I put myself into my work. I also met some men who disappointed me, but I believed that somewhere, sometime in my life, I would be happy again. A new chapter in my life was about to begin. It was going to be the most-clear, open, full-of-wonder, productive, and generous time I could ever have believed possible. I needed just to believe in me, in the power of the universe, and in the goodness of people. I had to surrender to everything that is good in me and let the force guide me.

Chapter 12
A New Life Chapter

The expense of Cyrus's treatment, including two major operations and almost a year's stay in a U.S. private hospital room, depleted our savings and more. Thanks to his life insurance policy, I was able to cover all expenses and had funds left to sustain me for a while without needing to liquidate my assets or change my lifestyle. I was aware, though, that soon I would need to plan for my future. I knew that my assets would not be enough to provide me with the lifestyle I was accustomed to. I needed to find a job that would provide me an income. I was forty-seven years old, and except for my volunteer work, I had no work experience for the past nineteen years.

I felt that my duty was to be an example for my children. I wanted them to see me as a strong woman, capable of taking control of the situation. I wanted them to learn that when confronted with tragedy or difficulties in life, it is necessary to assess the situation, evaluate the strengths within and around, look for opportunities, move on, and create a future. I wanted my children to have hope. I could feel their pain for the loss of their father and also their fear that Mom could not handle the situation. They had never experienced their mother in a position of control, managing a household, a business, or the family finances. I could see the doubt in their eyes, and it pained me.

The doubt in their eyes motivated me to act soon to prove to them that everything would be all right and that they could trust me. It was difficult to portray a sense of strength and self-assurance while my world was disintegrating. The future seemed so unpredictable and financially uncertain. Strangely, the future, with all its uncertainties, was also very appealing compared to the scary present.

I decided to embark on a new business venture: taking over Cyrus's insurance business where he had left it. I changed the type of business by opening a brokerage firm and employing brokers to work for me on commission. With the trust of various insurance companies, I ventured into unfamiliar territory. I had been an agent twenty-six years prior, but everything was different now, and I had never managed agents. The industry was dominated by men, especially in the management positions. I had my fears, but I knew that without taking a risk, nothing could be achieved.

I wanted to build a business where my children could work and make a living if they wished. When their father died, our younger son was in his second year of university and our older son was in his fourth year. The economy was not great at that time, and I thought establishing a business would give them an opportunity at least to have a job facilitated by a list of existing clients; the rest would be up to them. Both took advantage of the situation and worked several years in the business until they decided to find their own way and to fulfill their dreams. One found a job in an airline industry, which gave him the opportunity to do what he loved the most: traveling all over the world. The other, a born musician, is now a successful music composer and producer.

As for me, I was busy with my financial business, making good money, proving to myself that I could take care of myself and take care of others. I listened to my inherent wisdom that reminded me of my personal, academic, and professional accomplishments in life. I realized that in order to be successful in anything, I had to prepare myself, and I did so by acquiring the necessary skills to do the job. I also knew that in order to succeed, I needed four elements: need, desire, knowledge, and the determination to act.

After my children went their own ways, I continued my career in the financial business. For many years, I trained numerous brokers to become successful in their business, but I wanted more. I wanted to be true to myself. My business gave me financial security. My volunteer work had given me tremendous satisfaction in using my counseling skills, but I wanted to use my counseling skills in a different way, so I became a certified life coach and a mediator. I joined a collaborative law group in my city, and I am able now to work in a field that satisfies me intellectually and emotionally.

I am also a motivational speaker, spreading hope to all who feel trapped in someone else's idea of them and unable to honor their true selves. I speak to people who have lost hope about finding love again. I speak to women and men who have been abused and consequently are afraid to trust their selves and others. Abuse happens in all social classes and races. I believe it to be the most pervasive unrecognized social malady. It goes untreated, because the symptoms are usually hidden and the victims feel too ashamed to reveal their wounds. I decided to talk openly about my life, my experiences of abuse, and how I overcame my fears because being silent enables the abusers.

Many times I am asked, "What made you so strong to take actions in your life? Where did you find the strength to pick yourself up when confronted with adversities?" For someone it will be personal survival, the survival of one's individuality, and for others, it may be a combination of their individual freedom as well as their children's. It is our responsibility as mothers to save our children not only from physical harm but also from any harmful environment. For me, it was partly because I had no other choice—the alternative scared me—and partly because I started to believe that I had a choice.

I believe that in life we have choices, and problems occur when we forget that or when someone convinces us we have no right to choose. I consider free will a right of every human being. I believe that freedom of choice, together with life itself, is the most precious gift we have received from whatever deity we believe in. We work to keep ourselves alive, so we should maintain and exercise our right to choose.

When you are confronted by adversities in life, after doing your best to resolve them, you can consider them as opportunities to grow and to discover yourself, your strengths, and your weaknesses. I believe that a life without adversities is a life without growth. My best life lessons resulted from the challenges and tragedies I encountered. Not all circumstances in life are caused by your actions. How you choose to react to life's circumstances is up to you.

If you are in a relationship where you find yourself mostly in a defensive mode, you are well aware of the negative and painful emotions that arise by your partner's words, actions, or body language. Try preparing, in advance, a number of pleasant thoughts that you can summon up when that familiar painful feeling invades your mind and body. You can switch your thoughts to minimize your emotional reaction, allowing the problem-solving area of your brain to work. Become your best friend; protect yourself from any interference, which might prevent your growth and your ability to be true to yourself and to grow to your full potential.

Chapter 13

Loving Self, Loving Again

After Cyrus died, I felt an incredible loneliness. How could I live without a companion after sharing myself physically and emotionally for twenty-seven years? The absence of our habitual gestures and routines was a constant reminder that I was alone and that I could be alone for the rest of my life. The thought terrified me! With the exception of a few months when I first came to Canada, I had never been alone. I never had the opportunity to discover myself in my totality.

I missed having friends, my friends, to entertain Italian style: informally and with lots of fun. My entertainment had mostly been with Persian people, which was different than the Italian way; with the Persians it was less spontaneous, more formal. I always felt as if I had to perform my best and I would be judged how I entertained or cooked. I could understand that with less-close friends but I felt this way also with family.

I formed a group of six to eight single friends, men and women, from different cultures. We met every Saturday in each other's houses or in a restaurant. During the first dinner party I had in my home after Cyrus's death, I told them we would have an Italian dinner but that we would all make it together. I had wanted to do that for such a long time, and so I did. We put on Italian music and we opened a couple of bottles of wine.

Some made the salad; others cut the fresh bread while the muscles were cooking. The aromas filled the kitchen. Some of us started dancing and erupted in laughter. I could not believe the joy and the freedom I felt doing the simple things I had wanted to do for a long time. We sat down to a feast of spaghetti *alle vongole*, *zuppa di cozze*, and tiramisu while the stereo played Bocelli's romantic ballads. Oh, dear! How wonderful it was to enjoy a relaxing time with new and old friends, enjoying food and listening to familiar music. So simple, and yet it had been so foreign to me for a very long time.

I began to like my life, my freedom, my growth, and my successes. I had come a long way from the insecure, scared, semi-submissive person I was in the past, and I started to see the benefits of what my life had become. I was running a successful business managing a multitude of brokers. My children were having some growing pains, but I was confident in their abilities to learn from their experiences and eventually make the right decisions in their lives. I felt for the first time in my life that I knew myself. I was true to myself, and that gave me a lot of strength. I finally felt good about my life, and I was prepared to live it on my own, if that was my destiny.

With the encouragement and help of my friends, I started to date. Unfortunately, the men I met had as much or more baggage as I did. I felt romantically drained and I didn't have much to give. I was afraid that love would never come to me, but I also knew that I needed to feel love again. Realizing that I had never been loved the way I wanted to be loved and had never been accepted just as I was, I was afraid to open myself up to anyone and risk being disappointed again.

My first dating attempts were disastrous. I met men, some younger and some older than me, and they were all self-centered, completely lost, and looking for a mother or a daughter who would cater to their needs.

I was inexperienced. Times had changed and so had the dating scene. I fell for a man who satisfied me intellectually but was lacking emotionally. Both coming out of difficult marriages, we gravitated toward each other, seeking what each needed from a relationship at the time. I was craving intellectual stimulation, and he needed reassurance that he was lovable despite his inadequacies.

At the beginning of the relationship, I was unable to give of myself totally. I thought that as long as the physical and intellectual needs I had at the time were satisfied - I could be happy. Later in the relationship, though, I wanted more. I had started to open my heart, but he had no idea what love was. I finally realized that he was insecure about himself; he thought his wealth would compensate for his inadequacies in the relationship. He could love only himself and was unable to let anybody in. He eventually betrayed me with a friend who shared his love of money. At first I was hurt, as again I was experiencing betrayal, but after having enough time to reflect, I realized that it was the best thing to happen to me. It allowed me to find out what I did and did not want in a man. I wanted real love or nothing. But if love knocked at my door, would I recognize it and more importantly, was I ready for it?

Love Came Knocking

One day, an old friend whom I had not seen for a while introduced me to Giancarlo, a friend of her employer and frequent visitor at the travel agency where she worked. He was from Rome, and she thought we could be friends—or something else. My initial reaction was not a very favorable one, as my experiences with Italian men had not been very encouraging. My experience taught me that they like the chase, but when they catch you, they lose interest. This is the common description of Italian lovers by Italian women. Of course, not all Italian men are the same, but that was my impression at the time. Eventually, I started a friendly relationship with this man from Rome. Little did I know he would take me on a journey I had not planned but always dreamed of.

I always thought that when I met the man of my life, I would hear bells ringing and music playing, feel butterflies in my stomach, and everything else I had read in books. I also believed that if I did not instantly feel a connection with a person, I should conclude that the person is not the love of my life. When I met Giancarlo, I did not have butterflies in my stomach and I heard no bells, no music. To the contrary, I was put off by his near total silence. I am an extrovert, and he seemed a man of few words—a very few words.

We went to dinner together with my friend and her employer, accompanied by their respective spouses. We ate and talked but he was silent: not an attractive feature for a possible friendship. Little did I know that he was smitten with me, and that his silence was caused by the emotions he felt about me. In Italian we say, "*colpo di fulmine,*" which means "lightning strike." Oblivious of the reason for his silence, I decided not to see him again. Two days later, I received a package with flowers and a *panettone*, an Italian Christmas cake not available in Canada in November. During dinner, I had talked about my addiction to this cake, and he had arranged with his friend, the travel agent, to have the *panettone* brought immediately to Canada. In addition, he had a mini-*panettone* delivered to me every day for a month.

During that month we met frequently. My intention was only for a possible friendship, while he declared his romantic feelings one week to the day we met. He told me that I was the woman he had waited for all his life and he had known I was out there, but he feared he would never meet me. I was very surprised by his declaration of love, but I was more surprised by his answer when I commented that he couldn't possibly love me, as he did not know me at all.

He began listing my characteristics, my likes and dislikes, my hopes and dreams. I was shocked, but I did not lower my shield. I replied that some of the things he said were right, but still he did not really know me. I could not figure out how he knew so much about me. He described me with such conviction that it aroused my curiosity about this man whom I had met. As he courted me with flowers, chocolate, and *panettoni*, I thought: "Typical Italian; great at the chase." But, his insight about my true self kept me thinking. I continued to see him as a friend, and I told him I had no intention of starting a romantic relationship. As I continued to frequent him, I noticed his kindness, his multiple artistic talents, and his strength of character. He had been a smoker for thirty years, and he knew I did not approve his habit. He stopped smoking the week after I met him.

I was attracted also by his sense of humor. I realized how much I missed laughing with somebody without having to explain the jokes. We often referred to experiences we had lived and TV movies we had viewed during our lives in Italy, or to phrases we used which were parts of our lexicon. This was so attractive to me; it was like going home again.

We discovered that when we were in Rome, we lived only a few kilometers away from each other. We had frequented the same coffee shops and recreational establishments, walked through the same parks, watched the same TV shows, and laughed at the same jokes. He is just one year my senior, therefore we had grown up during the same period in Italy. I left Italy in 1966 -he left in 1980. There was so much I had missed, and he tried to fill in the gaps.

We discovered we both loved Canada very much, and that we wanted the same things from life: love, respect, commitment, and freedom to be ourselves with little regard for what other people thought. Giancarlo lived through a very difficult marriage and, due to his wife's diplomatic career and choices, found himself living most of his married life alone with his only son. I saw him as a misunderstood man, an artist who saw life through a magic-filtered lens; he could see only beauty and wanted to share his vision with the world. He was not allowed to do so, as his wings, like mine, were continually clipped by people around him who did not believe in his talent. When his wife received an appointment in Canada, he saw it as an opportunity, and he decided to leave Italy and move to his beloved Canada. He felt a strong pull toward life in North America ever since he had explored it years earlier during a vacation.

We were both trying to recover from painful situations in our respective lives, so at first we felt an incredible need to take care of each other's wounds. I experienced feelings I had never felt in a relationship before. I felt a comfort I had never felt before. When I fell in love before, I always felt a certain tension, mixed with excitement and fear, bundled up with all the other emotions that hormones provide and that I labeled as love. This time it was different. Everything fit. No effort, it felt so natural. I felt at home, in a safe place, embraced and rocked gently by firm and stable protective arms. I realized I had met love, and I became terrified. Is it true? Is it possible? Can I be fooled again? Can I trust my feelings, my mind, and my instincts? I was falling in love with Giancarlo, and it was too scary, too different from any feeling I had experienced in my life, so I ran.

I told Giancarlo that I did not think we were made for each other, and that I needed some time to think about my life and our relationship. I told him I needed at least a month to think and make a decision, and that I would get in touch with him when I was ready. How cold and mean I must have sounded to him. I wanted to reflect on what had happened between us and why I felt I had to stop the relationship. I thought I was getting too close, and I was terrified that I would be hurt again. I had defeated many of my demons but emotionally I had not healed.

I was getting used to the idea that I would not see him again when after only two weeks he called me, asking to meet with me for only a few minutes because he had something to give me. I reluctantly said yes, already deciding that I had lost interest in him because he did not stay true to our agreement to not communicate for a month. We went to a coffee shop, and after exchanging awkward kisses on the cheek he gave me a little package. He was shaking, and I knew he was very uncomfortable. I also knew that it had to do with my actions, and I felt very guilty. I proceeded to open the package in which I found a tiny book, the size of my thumb.

The title read, *Our Story*. Alternating pages contained a picture of a flower and printed words. He asked me to read it. The pages listed moments we had shared accompanied by his expression of the feelings that his knowing me had given him. He then declared his pain in not knowing how our story would end, and asked me to please hurry in writing the last chapter.

I was speechless, and tears streamed down from my eyes. All my fears left my heart. I saw a man in his fifties, ready to love me unconditionally, secure enough to be vulnerable with me, putting his heart in my hands. I realized that what I dreamed to find had been in front of my eyes for the last six months. I knew I was finally home. Love had finally caught me and I surrendered.

One day, while talking about my brother Paolo and his company in Italy, Giancarlo jumped up from his chair and started talking fast, "I knew there was something more. I have met you before in my life." I thought maybe he realized we met in Italy, but no. He reminded me we had met eighteen years earlier when he arrived in Canada with his wife and son. At my brother Paolo's request, I had invited Giancarlo and his family for tea. I answered my brother's request to be kind to his friend Giancarlo, who was moving to Canada with his family. Paolo asked me to help Giancarlo with information about life in Canada and Toronto. I invited the family for tea, we talked for a couple of ours, our children watched cartoons, and we never saw each other again, until we met eighteen years later.

I had not recognized him when I was introduced to him again years later, but I believe that if our families had established a relationship back then, I would have known a different Giancarlo, a Giancarlo reacting to different circumstances and married to another person. I was also different. We had to go through our challenges, defeat our demons, and when we were whole, destiny decided to let us meet.

Lessons Learned

The most important lesson my journey taught me is that the human spirit is strong. It can take an incredible amount of beating and still finds the strength to bounce back and carry us forward. I learned that love is always around you, but in order for it to embrace you, you must extend your arms.

I was reluctant to write this book, because it meant exposing myself to both people I know and to strangers. I know that regardless of my good intentions, talking about my life exposed the truth about the actors in it, and some people may feel hurt by it or misunderstand my intentions. A recurrent and insistent voice, though, kept telling me to write my story, as it would help other women who might identify with my experiences, and to tell them that there is hope and to have faith in the power of their inner wisdom. I needed to tell women: don't be afraid to make choices in your life—especially when your survival or your children's survival is at stake.

Things can happen that are out of your control, but your reactions to them will determine if you will be a victim or a victor. Build up your emotional strength to use along your life journey. Be the writer of your destiny, not just an actor. Believe in the ultimate power that will be with you through the journey to find and honor your true self. Remember that tomorrow is always the beginning of a new life.

Throughout it all, I never doubted the power of love. Love has always been present and a guide to my life decisions. I leave you with these quotations by Mahatma Gandhi and the Persian poet Hafiz that have touched me profoundly:

> *"Carefully watch your thoughts, for they become your words. Manage and watch your words, for they will become your actions. Consider and judge your actions, for they have become your habits. Acknowledge and watch your habits, for they shall become your values. Understand and embrace your values, for they become your destiny."*
>
> ~~ *Mahatma Gandhi*

> *Even after all this time the sun never says to the earth, "You owe me." Look what happens with a love like that, it lights the whole sky.*
>
> ~~ *Hafiz*

> *I wish I could show you when you are lonely or in darkness the astonishing light of your own being.*
>
> ~~ *Hafiz*

Vittoria Adhami, the founder and principal of *From Now On*," is a Life Coach, Professional Coach and Mediator. She is dedicated to helping people build strong personal, professional and community relationships. As a coach she has a background in psychology, mediation, hypnosis, and NLP, as well as other approaches to human development and change.

In her work with COSTI, which has provided services to millions of immigrants from all over the world, her goal is to help empower individuals and families to create productive lives in a new country. She is the chairperson of the women's program at COSTI. Along with being an immigrant from Italy herself, this work, over a period of many years, has allowed her to widen her understanding of cultural differences and further enrich her counseling skills.

In addition to being a Life Coach and Professional Coach, she is an associate of Halton-Peel Collaborative Law Group and a member of the International Academy of Collaborative Professionals. In addition, she owns and operates *Adhami & Adhami Financial Group*, an investment and insurance brokerage. As part of her dedication to community building she has been warranted the Ontario Volunteer Award, a very prestigious award in Canada.

Vittoria's discovery of Sharon Strand Ellison PNDC *Powerful Non-Defensive Communication*, has inspired her to teach its principles to Lawyers, Financial Professionals, Community Workers and Leaders in Canada. In addition, she has translated the PNDC program into Italian and she has brought PNDC to Italy.

To contact Vittoria for consulting or speaking to your organization check out her website:

http://fromnowon.ca/